90-Minute Fabric Fun

Terrie Kralik

©2006 Terrie Kralik

Published by

700 East State Street • Iola, WI 54990-0001
715-445-2214 • 888-457-2873

Our toll-free number to place an order or obtain
a free catalog is (800) 258-0929.

The following registered trademark terms, products and companies appear in this publication:
Bernina® of America, Clover Needlecraft Inc., Collins®, EZ Quilting®, June Tailor® Inc., Wrights®,
Fast2Fuse™, Graph 'n' Latch®, Olfa®, Prym® Consumer USA, Omnigrip®, Omnigrid®, Krause
Publications, Rowenta, Schmetz, Sulky® of America, The Warm™ Company, Timtex™, Annie's Attic,
Clotilde LLC, C&T Publishing, Connecting Threads, Herrschners Inc., Home Sew, Keepsake Quilting,
Nancy's Notions®, Baby Lock®, Brother®, Elna USA, Husqvarna® Viking® Sewing Machine Co., Janome,
White®, Kenmore®, Pfaff, Singer®, Tacony Corp., Lite Steam-A-Seam®, Lite Steam-A-Seam 2®.

Photo on page 3 was taken by Terrie Kralik.

Library of Congress Catalog Number: 2006929409

ISBN 13-digit: 978-0-89689-377-1

ISBN 10-digit: 0-89689-377-4

Designed by Heidi Bittner-Zastrow

Edited by Susan Sliwicki

Printed in the United States of America

Dedication

I dedicate this book to my family and friends.
Thanks for your constant encouragement
as I show you new ideas and finished projects
(and a few 'duds'). It's that kind of support
that feeds the creative spirit in me.

Acknowledgments

A special thank-you to the companies and employees who worked with me and provided fabric, various brands of stiff interfacing, fusible webs, locker hooking supplies, thread, notions and tools. When you have the right equipment and the best supplies available, you can't go wrong!

See the Contributors section at the end of the book for information about the specific products generously provided by these companies.

Thank you to my editor, photo and design teams who take a bunch of words, photos and ideas and work their magic to turn out a wonderful how-to book like this.

Thank you, Peaches, for sharing your locker hooking tricks with me. Thank you, JoAnn and Fonda, for your constant inspiration in all things fabric and quilted; and thank you, Darlene, for reviewing some of my directions for clarity.

And finally, thank you to the many fans I've met, either in person or by e-mail or phone. Your enthusiasm for my designs keeps me writing more!

Introduction

Welcome to the fun world of playing with fabric! I'm glad you've decided to join me. I have a book full of projects to share with you, and I intend to keep sewing interesting and fun.

You won't find the traditional quilts and wall hangings here, but any sewing or quilting experience you have may still apply. If you are new to sewing, directions are clear and concise just for you, with a lot of diagrams and pictures.

I've compiled a variety of projects that range from locker-hooked trivets to boxes and bowls made with fabric-covered interfacing. Sewing has been kept to a minimum, and some projects are made totally without a sewing machine. Others will require that you be able to sew a zigzag stitch or straight stitch on your machine, but nothing fancier than that. When you find a technique that you truly enjoy (and you want to do more), look for the larger and more difficult projects that use the same technique.

I recommend that you use rotary cutting equipment and rulers, but precision isn't critical. These are all good projects to get experience using your tools.

Chapters are divided by technique. All of the locker-hooked items are together, all of the boxes and "boxy" containers are together, and all of the bowls are together. Thorough directions for each technique start each chapter. Even if you are familiar with a technique, check out the tons of tips. Chances are you'll still find something new or helpful!

Take a few minutes to try one project, and I bet you will be hooked… or boxed in, or bowled over. Enjoy yourself!

Terrie.

About the Author

An avid quilter, Terrie Kralik has taught quilting for more than 15 years. She began publishing her own quilting patterns in 1997 through her company, Moose Country Quilts, and she has written two quilting how-to books, "A Forest of Quilts" and "Quilted Forest Décor." She enjoys experimenting with new designs and techniques with fabric and sharing her knowledge with others. Kralik lives in Idaho with her family. Visit her Web site at www.MooseCountryQuilts.com.

Table of Contents

Chapter 4: Bowls........................ 112

CHAPTER 1

Begin

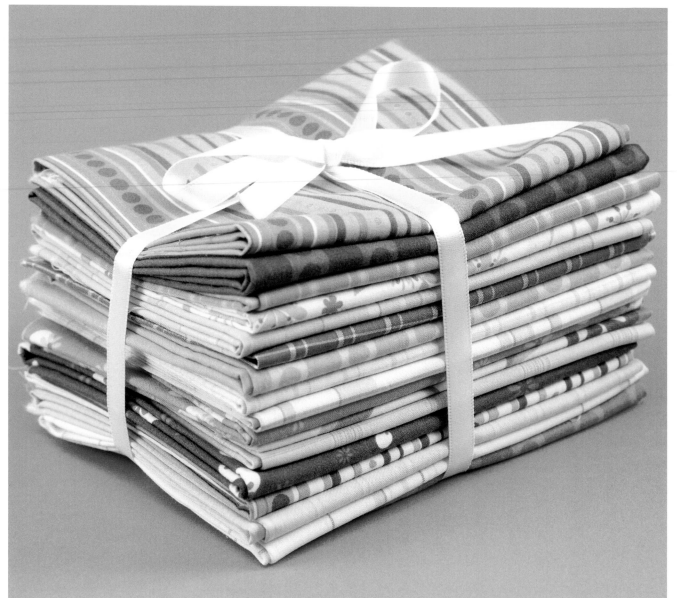

Let's begin at the beginning. Here are basic tips and information about sewing, fabrics, tools and supplies. Consult the Glossary at the back of the book for definitions.

General Tools and Supplies

Having the right tools makes the difference between having fun while you sew these projects and fighting with your equipment. Use the best tools available to you.

Sewing Machine and Accessories

Almost any sewing machine is sufficient to sew these projects, as long as it is able to sew a zigzag stitch and is in good working order. The age of your machine is not as much a factor as how it has been maintained. If you can't remember when it was last oiled or serviced by a knowledgeable technician, take it in for a tune-up, just like you would a car. A little sewing machine maintenance up front will avoid major breakdowns further down the road. (Sewing machines always seem to have problems when you have a deadline to meet and no time to spare!)

Begin with a sharp sewing machine needle, and keep extras on hand. I generally use a size 80/12 needle unless I'm using a specialty thread that calls for a different size. Projects that require a lot of zigzag stitching will produce lint in your machine rapidly, and poor thread will add to this condition. Remove lint from your machine frequently; oil your machine often, as well. Your sewing machine manual will tell you what maintenance you can do and how often, and what must be done by a technician.

While a standard sewing machine presser foot will work fine, you may find it helpful to use a walking or darning foot to quilt layers of fabric in the larger projects, such as the boxes.

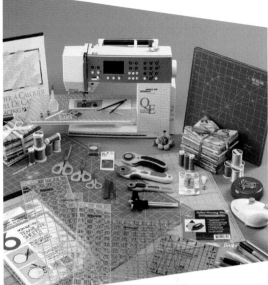

General sewing, cutting and pressing tools and supplies.

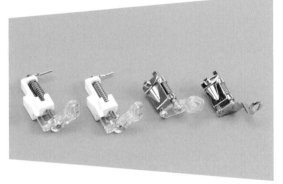

Darning feet.

Walking feet.

Cutting Tools

A good pair of fabric scissors are handy to snip threads or make small cuts. But when it comes to cutting and trimming projects, I prefer to use a 45 mm rotary cutter for ease and accuracy. I keep a fresh blade in it at all times. A smaller rotary cutter may be fine, too, especially for cutting tight curves.

If you are just starting to use rotary equipment and have to purchase everything new, start with a standard 45 mm rotary cutter, an 18" x 24" self-healing cutting mat, a 6" x 12" ruler and 6" x 24" ruler. Other rulers and equipment can follow. There are so many different brands of rulers and cutters available, I suggest that you go to a craft or quilt shop and ask to try out each. You may find that one rotary cutter fits your hand easier, or that a certain brand of ruler is easier to read.

Once you have your equipment, use only your own tools so you can get comfortable with them. The locker hooking projects use many fabric strips cut with your rotary cutter; they are an excellent project to start with.

Pressing Tools

You will need an ironing board and an iron that can press both with and without steam. Protect your ironing board by covering it with muslin, or press your projects on top of a nonstick pressing sheet.

A tailor's ham and a miniature iron also will come in handy, particularly for the box projects.

Notions and Other Supplies

Hand sewing needles may be needed on some projects, so I suggest having a package of needles in a variety of sizes. As you become more adept at using them, you may find that one size may be too big, another too small, and another perfect for a little heavier thread. You may also find a thimble useful when hand sewing.

Straight and safety pins also are useful for these projects. Whether you like glass-head, flower-head or quilting pins, the key is to choose clean, sharp pins designed for use with fabric. A magnetic or other style of pincushion will keep your pins from straying.

Use high-quality thread in colors to match or contrast your project, according to your preference. I have a wonderful collection of threads from which to choose, including variegated threads of different weights, cottons, rayons and cotton-covered polyesters. Old threads may be too brittle to use, so use fresh and new product. Standard-weight thread is great to start with, and projects that require something different will specify what to use.

Finally, I hate to say it, but you will need a seam ripper in your collection of tools, too. And here again, there is a huge variety of brands and styles. Find one that is sharp with a good point and one that fits your hand comfortably. Mine is quite experienced, and is from my sewing classes in middle school!

In addition to hand sewing needles, thread, pins, safety pins and a seam ripper, you may need:

- Tracing paper;
- Template plastic;
- Glue stick;
- A small clamp;
- Binder clips; and
- Rubber bands or elastic ponytail bands.

Locker-Hooking Supplies

Rug canvas is used in the locker hooking projects. It comes in different sizes and brands. The projects shown here all use a 3.75 grid canvas with a blue line printed on it at specific intervals. It is heavier and firmer than some other brands, which makes it easier to work with.

Also used with locker hooking is a cotton string-like thread called twine. It comes either in a skein or cone by one company or pre-cut in 36" lengths from another company.

In addition to rug canvas, twine and general sewing tools and supplies, you'll also need:

- A locker hook, which has a hook at one end and an eye at the other;
- Needle nose pliers; and
- A blunt tapestry or needlepoint needle.

Check the Contributors at the back of the book for specific products and where to purchase them. Most of these items are available by mail order or on the Internet, if you can't find them locally.

Box and Bowl-Making Supplies

You'll need stiff interfacing to complete the bowl and box projects. One product (Fast2Fuse) has fusible web glue on both surfaces, while the other (Timtex) does not; they also come in different weights, widths and packaging. If only one of these products is best for a project, it will be listed. Otherwise, you may use either one. When using the product without fusible web, you may need to purchase a fusible web separately and add it where specified in the directions; or use an alternate method, such as a glue stick or temporary spray adhesive. I prefer to use Timtex with a glue stick. Check with your local craft or quilt shop, or see the Contributors listed at the back of the book for other options.

In addition to stiff interfacing, fusible web, glue stick, spray adhesive and general sewing tools and supplies, you may also need:

- Pinking shears or decorative-edge scissors;
- A miniature iron;
- A tailor's ham or everyday items, such as cardboard boxes, baking pans or mixing bowls;
- Circle patterns, such as bucket lids, jar lids, tins, embroidery hoops and dinner plates;
- Oval patterns, such as platters, wicker baskets and picture mats and frames;
- Embroidery floss, cording and embellishments.

Locker-hooking supplies.

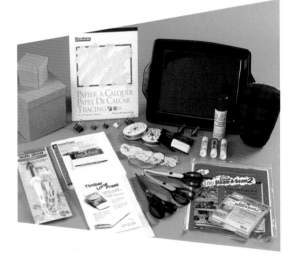

Box and bowl-making supplies.

TOOLS AND SUPPLIES AT A GLANCE

Here's a quick checklist of the items you'll want to have handy when you are creating the projects featured in this book. Refer to each project's materials list for detailed pattern and fabric information.

Bowl and Box Making
- ☐ Stiff interfacing
- ☐ Fusible web
- ☐ Glue stick
- ☐ Pinking shears or decorative-edge scissors
- ☐ Miniature iron
- ☐ Tailor's ham
- ☐ Mixing bowls
- ☐ Cardboard boxes

Cutting
- ☐ 45 mm rotary cutter with spare blade
- ☐ 18" x 24" cutting mat
- ☐ 6" x 12" and 6" x 24" clear acrylic rotary cutting rulers
- ☐ Fabric scissors

Embellishing
- ☐ Cording
- ☐ Ribbon
- ☐ Buttons
- ☐ Beads
- ☐ Trim
- ☐ Yarn
- ☐ Embroidery thread

Pressing
- ☐ Iron
- ☐ Ironing Board
- ☐ Nonstick pressing sheet or muslin
- ☐ Bowls, boxes, a tailor's ham, etc.

Locker Hooking
- ☐ Rug canvas
- ☐ Locker hook
- ☐ Twine

General Notions
- ☐ Seam ripper
- ☐ Tracing paper
- ☐ Template plastic
- ☐ Glue stick
- ☐ Small clamp
- ☐ Binder clips
- ☐ Rubber bands

Sewing
- ☐ Sewing machine with spare sewing machine needles
- ☐ Standard-weight thread and decorative thread
- ☐ Straight pins and pincushion
- ☐ Safety pins
- ☐ Hand sewing needles in various sizes
- ☐ Thimble

Fabric

I have used high-quality, 100 percent cotton fabric in all the projects shown, but other fabrics may work equally well. Tightly woven fabrics will give you great results in all box and bowl projects. Avoid — or stabilize — loosely woven fabrics, because they fray and distort easily.

Fabrics make a statement. Your choice of fabrics for these projects will give it your personal touch and show off your individual flair. Use novelty prints to make bowls and boxes for a playful look. More elegant fabrics will give a romantic, Victorian or cultured look to your projects. Country colors and prints will add a rustic charm. A large print will create a completely different look than a small print of similar coloration, and geometric prints may look unlike anything you planned once they are sewn or hooked into your project.

For many of the containers shown, I used simple or near-solid fabrics to offset prints. Since most bowls are reversible, this gave two distinct looks with no extra work! Boxes and other containers that are not reversible usually have a simpler print or solid inside to give them a more professional-looking appearance.

Speaking of looking professional, remember to trim all of your threads as you go. This will keep your project neat and tidy, and you won't be trying to cover up those loose ends constantly.

Sewing Tips

Most projects featured in this book are very fast to make, but others may take a little longer to do. If you find that you like a certain type of project, such as locker hooking, it might be fun to try a more-complicated or larger-size project, so I've included some of these more difficult projects. Read the notes with each project to find out how difficult it is to make.

Technique and project tips appear throughout the book, but here are some basic rules of thumb to follow for every project:

- Use high-quality products.
- Cut the largest pieces of your project first, whether

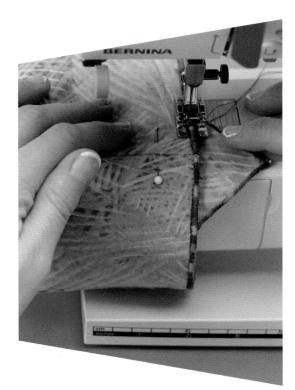

they are cut from stiff interfacing or fabric. Smaller pieces can be cut from the remaining yardage.

- Cut and trim pattern pieces accurately.
- Sew a ¼" seam unless otherwise indicated.
- Sew with a standard stitch length of about 2.
- Backstitch as indicated in the instructions.
- Trim threads and frayed fabric as you go.
- Test new products or fabric combinations in some way before using them in your project.

Embellishments

The sky is the limit when it comes to embellishing your projects. A variety of ready-made trims, tassels, baubles and fibers are available at your local fabric and craft shops. I have added buttons to one project, but beads, yarn, ribbon and other trims are just as easy to add. Once you start embellishing, your projects will call out for something special. Just have fun!

Braided Trim
Supplies
Fabric
Binder clips
Rubber bands or elastic hair ties
General tools and supplies

TIP

- As a general rule, 1"-wide fabric strips will make a braid that measures about ½" wide; 1½"- wide strips make a ⅝"-wide braid; and 2"-wide strips make a ¾"-wide braid. Of course, if you braid very tightly, the finished braid width will vary some. Finally, the finished braid will be about two-thirds of the length of the original strips. For example, a 40" strip of fabric will yield a 26" length of braid.

Cut

From	Size	How Many	For
Braid fabric	Strips, as directed in your project; remove the selvages after cutting	Number directed in your project	Braided Trim

Construct

1. If you need to make longer strips, use a ¼" seam to sew the strips right sides together at the narrow ends of the strips; press the seams open. Otherwise, proceed to Step 2.

2. Press the strips in half, wrong sides together; each strip will now be half of its original width but still the same length.

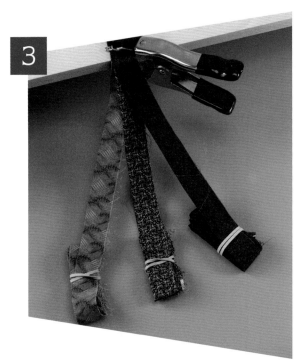

3. Safety pin three strips together at one end; use a binder clip or another clamping device to clamp the strips to a stationary surface, like a desk or table (or a stationary friend). Wrap the extra length of strips with rubber bands or elastic hair ties to keep the strips from tangling.

4. Braid the length needed, or until you run out of strips. Re-clamp the braid often, and work fairly close to your clamp (not across the room). Keep a uniform tension as you braid, and keep your movements consistent.

5. Pin the end of your braided length. Machine stitch across each braid end; backstitch at the beginning and end of stitching, or simply sew a second line of stitching over the first line. Use thread to match your fabric.

6. Trim the excess braid to about ⅛" from the stitched line.

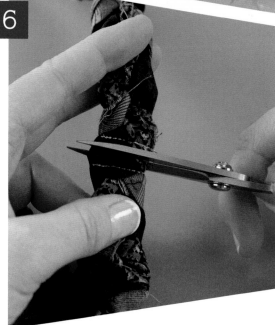

TIP

• To cut more than one piece from a single length of braid (such as for two handles), first stitch on both sides of where you plan to cut; leave ⅜" between stitching lines. Now cut the braid apart. If you cut it first and then sew, chances are that your braid will unravel.

Variation: Braid as Trim or Handles

1. Make the length of braid as directed in the project instructions.

2. Position the braid on the project as shown to make sure it is long enough. Do not trim the braid to the to exact length at this time. Decide where to begin and end the braid; an inconspicuous spot is best. Use binding clips to temporarily hold the braid in place.

3. Sew the braid by hand or machine, tacking the braid every 1½" to 2". On bowls, tack at each sewn seam and at least once between seams; on handles, tack in at least two places on each braid end. By hand, sew through the braid and the project; use doubled thread and knot it at the beginning and end. By machine, zigzag stitch the braid in place with feed dogs dropped.

4. About 2" to 3" before your ending point, determine the exact length of braid needed, and mark this with a pin. Stitch by machine across the braid a bit before this pin and again on the other side of the pin if you plan to use the remaining braid. Cut the braid between the stitching lines.

5. Finish tacking the rest of the braid in place. Take extra stitches where the braid ends meet, and anchor them well.

Tassels

Supplies (for one tassel)

2 skeins of six-strand embroidery floss
Cardboard
Embroidery needle or other needle with a large eye
Fine-tooth comb
General tools and supplies

Cut

From	Size	How Many	For
Cardboard	The size specified in the project; for example, to make a 3" tassel, the cardboard must measure 3" in at least one direction (i.e. 3" x 6", 3" x 3", 2" x 3")	1	Tassel form
Embroidery floss	7" length 12" length	1 1	Tassel tie and hanger Tassel wrap

Construct

I. Use the embroidery floss as it comes out of the package, with all six strands intact. Begin wrapping embroidery floss around the cardboard, with the tail at the bottom of cardboard; this will be the bottom of your tassel. Wrap the embroidery floss around the cardboard the number of times listed in the project or to your personal preference. Note that each time around the cardboard is called a wrap.

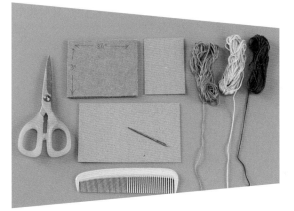

2. Trim the end of the embroidery floss so it is a bit longer than the first tail, again ending at the bottom of the tassel.

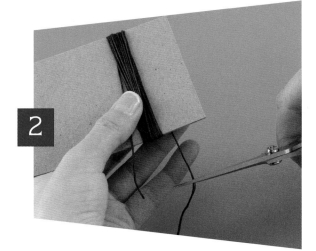

3. Thread the needle with a 7" length of embroidery floss, and pull the floss between the cardboard and tassel wraps on one side.

4. Pull the floss so the tie ends are equal.

5. Remove the needle, and knot the floss tightly around the strands at the top of the tassel.

6. Slip the wrapped floss off of the cardboard. Don't cut anything.

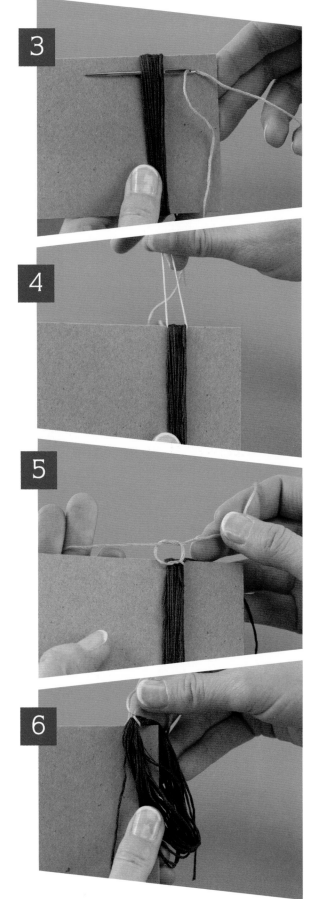

7. Use the 12" length of embroidery floss to wrap the upper edge of the tassel as shown. Remember the process this way: Loop, wrap, thread and tug.

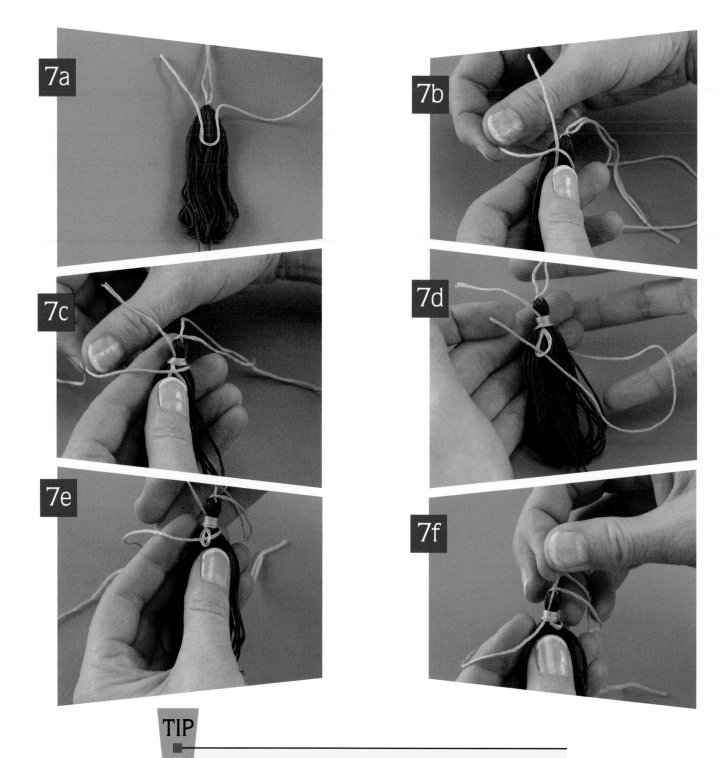

7a
7b
7c
7d
7e
7f

TIP

I like to remember the tassel-making process as Loop, Wrap, Thread and Tug. I usually make six to nine wraps in this process.

8. Trim both ends of the tassel wrap as shown; be sure to leave two long strands of the tassel tie to be used later to create a hanger.

9. Cut the loops at the bottom edge of the tassel.

10. Comb out the embroidery floss with a fine-tooth comb; hold the upper part of the tassel firmly as you comb.

11. Trim the tassel so the bottom edge is even.

12. Use the two long strands of embroidery floss left from the tassel wrap to create your tie. Your tassel is ready to attach to your project.

TIP

Use variegated floss or several colors together to add a distinctive touch to your tassels.

Bows

Supplies

1 spool (at least 3 yd.) craft ribbon,
  at least ⅞" wide*

Lightweight floral or beading wire

Wire cutters

General tools and supplies

*Note: You can use either wired or unwired ribbon to make this type of bow.

Cut

1. Trim each end of the ribbon at an angle to prevent fraying.

Construct

1. About 8" from one end of the ribbon, make a 5" to 6" loop. Pinch the center of the loop firmly between your finger and thumb.

TIP

Add a stylish accent with this easy-to-make bow. It's the perfect way to turn a lidded fabric box into a keepsake gift box.

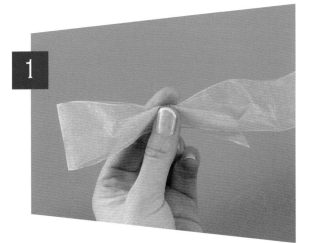

2. Continue to create 5" to 6" loops, striving to keep them a uniform size.

3. Make a few more loops.

4. Once all of the loops are made, use wire to tie off the bow and hold it in place.

5. Adjust the loops as desired.

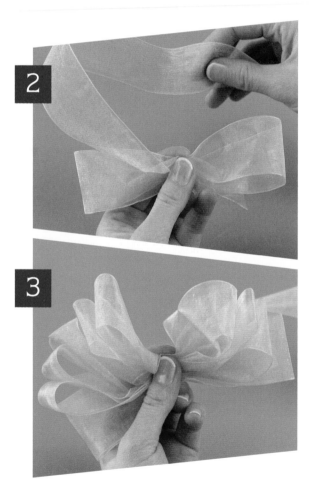

CHAPTER 2

Mats

Locker hooking is a relaxing, even mesmerizing, technique that combines fabric strips, rug canvas and a hooking process similar to crocheting. I have to warn you, though: This is addictive. With that in mind, I've included simple designs that are perfect for your first experience with locker hooking, plus more advanced projects. Most designs are easily adaptable to other shapes and sizes. For each project, refer to the tips and detailed instructions at the beginning of the chapter.

Locker Hooking Tips

Terms

• The term "round" refers to hooking in a circular pattern (clockwise or counterclockwise) around a certain area or around the canvas perimeter. For example, three rounds means you will hook around the project three times, like jogging around a track three times.

• The term "row" refers to hooking in a back-and-forth motion; each line of stitching is a single row. Think of this as pacing back and forth, right to left.

Canvas

• Two different sizes of rug canvas are available. The projects shown in this book are all made with the smaller 3.75 size. There are 3.75 grids per inch of canvas.

• There is no right or wrong side to the canvas.

• Not all canvases are equal; some are firmer than others, and some include a colored grid to help with pattern work. The stiffer canvas is easier to work with, and the colored grid can be very helpful. My favorite is Graph 'n' Latch canvas by M.C.G. Textiles. All of the projects in this book were made using this canvas.

Twine

• Cotton twine is used instead of polyester yarn because it does not stretch and is strong and stable.

Fabric

• Locker-hooked projects use a lot of fabric. This is a great way to use outdated or scrap fabrics. Only the overall color of a fabric shows, not the complete design. Test each to see what it will look like.

• Fabrics that have nearly the same color on the right side and wrong side create a more consistent look with less work than others do.

• Remove the selvages from the strips before using them in your project.

• I prefer to work with 1½"-wide strips of high-quality

Locker hooking tools.

Fabric strips.

cotton fabric, but 1¼"-wide strips are also usable. The fabric thickness and your hooking style will affect your work; choose a width that fills the space to your liking. Like knitting or crocheting, beginners will start with one size of stitch and gradually work into a more uniform and consistent stitch.

• Cut lightweight fabric into wider strips to fill the space better. Cut heavier denim, upholstery-weight or fleece fabrics in narrow strips. Test stitch a short length of your fabric strip to find the proper width needed for the project.

Hooking

• Test hook a strip to see how it will look, both to verify the proper strip width and to decide if the colors work as expected. Start a small canvas piece for test strips.

• Hooked stitches change with practice; warm up on a practice piece, like your small test strip piece.

• Work with fabric strips below the canvas; twine and hook above the canvas.

• Try to have knots and splices anywhere in your project except at the corners.

• As you hook each loop, pull the fabric strips to a uniform height on the front. Each stitch on the back should lay flat.

• Remember that the outer two or three rows of your project are the hardest to hook.

• It doesn't matter if you hook in a clockwise or counter-clockwise direction.

• To remove hooked areas right after you've stitched them, work from the surface of your project. Pull out the twine between loops; then pull out the fabric from the backside or underside.

• The direction of hooking does matter in the overall pattern, and it can be an integral part of the project's design. Think of this as paint strokes, where you can see the direction each stroke follows.

• Hold your mouth just right and make a funny face, and you'll find the whole process is easier. Yes, at first you will feel like a kid learning to ride a bike. It gets easier, though, and you'll be addicted before you know it.

TIP

It's easy to figure out how much fabric you need to create a design of your own.

1. Cut the canvas at least 1" larger than the dimensions of your finished piece. For example, cut a 10" square canvas piece for a 9" square finished project.

2. Calculate your fabric needs. One strip of fabric, approximately 40" to 42" long, will fill about 8" of a single row of hooked stitches.

3. Determine how many 8" lengths you have per row.

4. Multiply the number determined in Step 3 by the number of total rows.

5. Multiply the number determined in Step 4 by the width of your fabric strips to yield the number of inches of fabric you need.

6. Divide the number determined in Step 5 by 36 to yield the total yardage required for your project.

Test piece.

Splicing

• Change colors and splice fabric strips without a lot of loose ends with this process. Hook up to and including the last loop of the design before changing fabrics; trim away the fabric even with or slightly longer than the underside of project, leaving the twine intact. Now, remove the last three stitches you just made; cut a blunt point and slit in this fabric tail. Splice with the new fabric and continue hooking. Adjust where you trim this so that the knot and new color begin exactly where you expect it to.

Finishing

• The hardest part of locker hooking is finishing off the ends so everything is neatly hidden, yet permanently attached somehow. There aren't a lot of rules here, so use your imagination and skills from other craft projects to your advantage.
• Use needle-nose pliers or a blunt tapestry needle to adjust the loop height as needed.
• Overcast stitching the outer edge of your project is optional, but it adds a beautiful finish.

Locker Hooking Directions

1. Remove the selvage from the canvas. Then, cut the rug canvas to the size specified. There is no need to trim away the excess nubs on the canvas edge.

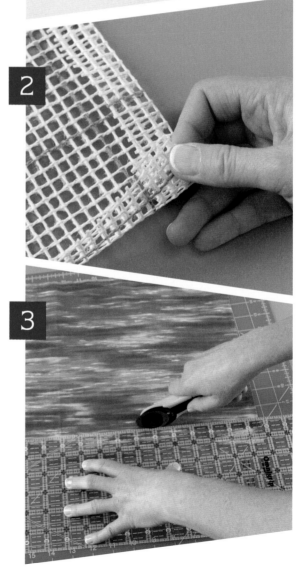

2. Fold three or more grids to the underside of the canvas, overlapping and lining up holes. (The canvas has no right or wrong side.) For larger projects, overlap four or more rows. Repeat this on all sides; pin the folded rows in place with safety pins if needed. Note: The corners will be bulky.

3. Cut fabric into strips, usually 1¼" or 1½" wide (see Tips). Remove the selvages. Note that the yardage amount varies by project and is just an estimate. Yardage amounts are based on 1½" wide × 42" long strips.

4. Refer to the Fabric Preparation Diagram. Trim the ends of each fabric strip to a blunt point. Cut a ⅜"-long slit near each point in preparation for splicing. Do this by folding the point downward over the fabric strip about ½"; clip through the fold as shown. Open up the strip; it is ready to use.

TIP

Cut the fabric strips from selvage to selvage or along the straight of grain (parallel to the selvage). Any length of strip will work, but keep in mind you may have a small bump at every fabric splice, so more pieces equals more splices and more bumps.

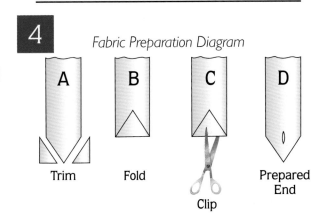

Fabric Preparation Diagram

4

| A | B | C | D |
| Trim | Fold | Clip | Prepared End |

5. Work with 36" lengths of twine. Anchor one end of twine to the canvas with a double-knot placed on an outer edge and near the center of that side; leave a 4" tail that will be worked in later. If you should start in another position on the canvas, your project directions will tell you this.

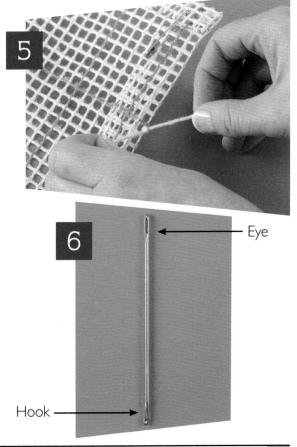

Eye

6. Thread the free end of twine through the eye of your hook, as you would thread a needle.

Hook

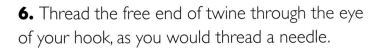

7. Begin hooking fabric strips to the canvas, leaving a 4" fabric tail. This will be worked in later. Hold the fabric strip below the canvas (the underside), and work with the hook and twine from above (the surface or right side of the project).

8. Take the hook tool through an open grid in the canvas next to your starting knot. Catch the fabric strip below, pull it through the grid to the surface of your project, and slide the "stitch" back on the hook. Repeat. Hook one to 10 stitches at a time, depending on your comfort level, then pull the twine through these loops and repeat. This motion is like a combination of crocheting and hand sewing.

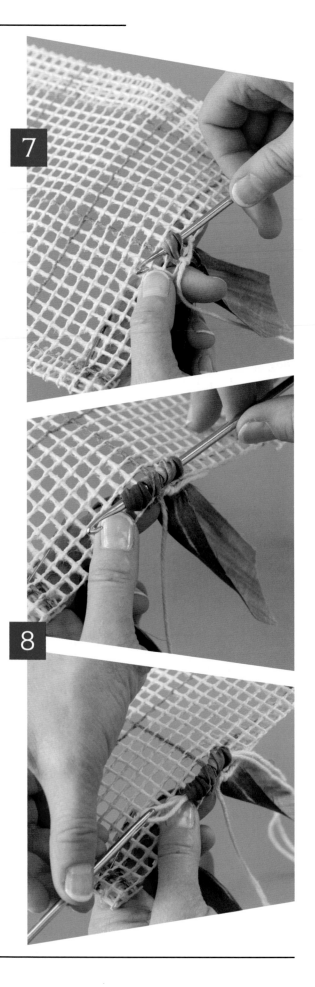

TIP

One way to work with strips is to fold fabric in half or thirds, with the print right side out and raw edges tucked in. Do this with one hand under the project before pulling the strip through with the hook. Another way to work with fabric strips is to hook with a uniform height, paying no mind to the raw edges the right or wrong sides of the fabric or how it naturally folds.

9. Hook around the perimeter of your canvas, repeating until you have three or four rows of a hooked frame. This stabilizes the rest of the canvas.

10. To splice twine, refer to the Twine Splicing Diagram. Use an overhand knot or square knot (shown) to join the old and new pieces of twine. Trim the splice to a ½" tail.

Twine Splicing Diagram

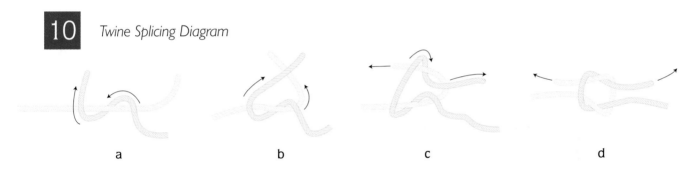

a   b   c   d

11. To splice fabric strips, refer to the Fabric Splicing Diagram. Begin with fabric strips that are already prepared. Then overlap the points, right side up, so one point is upward and one point is downward. Line up the clipped openings. Poke the point of the new strip through the slit in the old strip, and pull the tail clear through.

Fabric Splicing Diagram

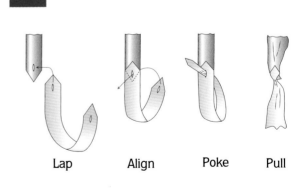

Lap   Align   Poke   Pull

12. If you are working in rows, skip to Step 13. If you are working in **rounds**, complete the round as usual, pulling the twine through your last stitch. To continue on the next round, take the hook and twine (no fabric) downward through the grid just past your last stitch, then diagonally upward through the open grid, one stitch back. The twine will now pull against the grid rather than against your last fabric stitch.

13. If you are working in **rows**, complete the row as usual, pulling the twine through your last stitch. To continue on the next row, take the hook and twine (no fabric) downward through the grid, just past your last stitch, and then upward through the grid in the next row, just outside where you want to continue. This will anchor your twine, and it will pull against the grid rather than tug at the fabric stitch and show the twine.

TIP

Remember the fabric splicing process with this easy mnemonic device: LAPP. It stands for lap, align, poke and pull.

1. LAP: Overlap the point of the new strip over the end of the old strip; points will face in opposite directions with both fabrics right side up. Place the old strip pointing downward, and new strip pointing upward, on top.

2. ALIGN: Line up the clipped openings. Hold this with one hand.

3. POKE: Poke the point of the tail of the new strip through the clipped opening in the strips you are holding.

4. PULL: Pull tail clear through and tug until the splice is snug and tight; straighten out the points as needed.

14. Hook the design as directed, changing colors or fabric strips as needed or desired.

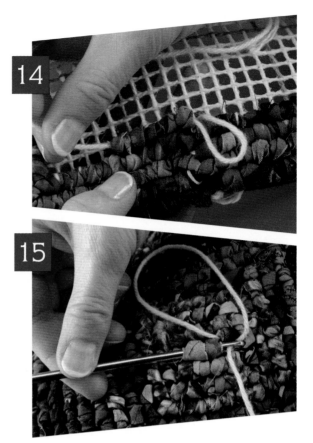

15. End the last stitch on your project. Leave a 4" fabric tail and 6" twine tail; trim away the rest. Cut the fabric tail to a point to reduce bulk.

TIP

To end a color or fabric strip at a certain point and continue with another, hook the design, including the last stitch you want of the current fabric, but don't pull the twine through the last three stitches. Leave your hook through these three loops. Turn the project over, and trim the excess fabric strip even with the back, cutting straight across. Remove the hook, and pull out those last three stitches. Trim the fabric strip end to a point, and cut a slit for splicing. Splice another strip, then continue hooking.

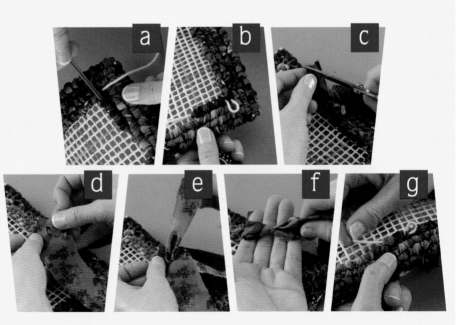

16. Use a tapestry needle to bring all of the twine and fabric ends to the surface of your project.

16

17. Anchor and hide the twine tails. Work from the project surface and use the tapestry needle. Choose one of these options:
a) Wrap the twine around the canvas between hooked loops several times; pull the last bit through fabric loops and trim off. OR,
b) Wrap and knot the twine around canvas; pull the remaining twine through fabric loops and trim off. OR,
c) Wrap and knot the twine around the fabric tail; pull the remaining length of both through fabric loops and trim off.

TIP

If your fabric pulls through and rips out when you tug the splice tight, cut a new point at that end. Fold over a bit more fabric than before, and cut a clip. Why did this happen? The clip was too long or too close to the point of the fabric.

17

18. Anchor and hide the fabric tails. Work from the project surface and use the tapestry needle. Trim the fabric tail to a sharper point than for splicing. Next, choose one of these options:
a) Thread each tail through several fabric loops on the surface of your project, changing direction if possible. OR,
b) Wrap and knot the twine around the fabric tail, pulling this as a unit through several loops and trimming off the excess. Hint: if you do needle-point or cross-stitch, the anchoring process is similar.

TIP

For stability and longer life, tie or anchor each loose end rather than just tucking it in somewhere. If needed, use a pair of needle-nosed pliers to pull the needle. Problem areas can be stitched or tacked by hand with a standard needle and thread.

19. If desired, overcast stitch the outer edge of project to cover the raw canvas. From leftover fabric, cut strips that are half the width used in your project and no more than 20" long. For example, overcast with ¾"-wide strips if the project used 1½"-wide strips for locker hooking. Use a tapestry needle or locker hook with the fabric strip only; there is no twine in this stitch. Leave a 3" tail at the beginning; fold it toward your next few stitches so it can be caught in this wrap. Wrap in an overhand motion, stitching in each grid space. Another option is to anchor and hide each loose tail after all of the edges have been overcast.

20. Anchor the final tail of fabric by reversing the direction of your overcast stitching, then stitch through three grids, or hiding the tail inside the last few wraps; trim the excess.

TIP

When you are overcast stitching the edges of the mat, keep the fabric strip length shorter, because pieces will quickly fray and almost fall apart in this process. Keep the fabric strips flat as you wrap for best coverage. The corners may require extra stitches to cover them properly. Splice the fabric pieces the same as other strips, or just overlap the stitches and the loose tail the same as at the beginning of the overcast stitching.

Mama Trivet

Finished size: 11" x 11" (40 x 40 grid). Shown with scrap braided coasters, Flip Top Box and Square Basket with Braided Trim.

Supplies

12" × 12" rug canvas
Cotton locker hooking twine
1½ yd. various dark green prints
⅔ yd. dark pansy print
½ yd. purple solid or near solid
½ yd. yellow solid or near solid
Locker hook
Blunt tapestry or needlepoint needle
Needle-nose pliers, optional
General tools and supplies

Cut

From	Size	How Many	For
Dark green prints	1½"-wide strips, or your preferred width	As many as yardage allows	Perimeter, center
Dark pansy print	1½"-wide strips, or your preferred width	As many as yardage allows	Inner rows
Purple solid	1½"-wide strips, or your preferred width	As many as yardage allows	Inner rows
Yellow solid	1½"-wide strips, or your preferred width	As many as yardage allows	Inner rows

Construct

1. Fold the raw edge of the canvas under three rows, overlapping and aligning the openings.

2. Hook three rounds of dark green print around the perimeter of the rug canvas; use a circular pattern. Mix and match fabrics or repeat a single fabric. Refer to the Mama Trivet Construction Diagram.

3. Hook one round of purple solid.

4. Hook three rounds of dark green print.

5. Hook two rounds of yellow solid.

6. Hook three rounds of dark pansy print.

7. Hook one round of purple solid.

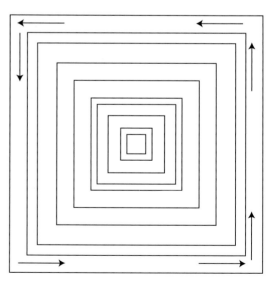

Mama Trivet Construction Diagram

8. Hook two rounds of dark green prints.

9. Hook two rounds of dark pansy print.

10. Hook one round of yellow solid.

11. Hook the remaining center area with dark green prints.

12. Overcast stitch the outer edge of the canvas.

13. Tie off all of the loose tails.

Baby Trivet

Finished size: 9" x 9" (35 x 35 grid).

Supplies

10" x 10" rug canvas
Cotton locker hooking twine
1 yd. dark green print
½ yd. medium-dark purple print
¼ yd. light purple print
Locker hook
Blunt tapestry or needlepoint needle
Needle-nose pliers, optional
General tools and supplies

Cut

From	Size	How Many	For
Dark green print	1½"-wide strips, or your preferred width	As many as yardage allows	Perimeter
Medium-dark purple print	1½"-wide strips, or your preferred width	As many as yardage allows	Inner rows, center
Light purple print	1½"-wide strips, or your preferred width	As many as yardage allows	Inner rows

Construct

1. Fold the raw edge of the canvas under three rows, overlapping and aligning the grid openings.

2. Hook eight rounds of dark green print around the perimeter of the rug canvas; follow a circular pattern. Mix and match fabrics, or repeat a single fabric, if desired. Refer to the Baby Trivet Construction Diagram.

3. Hook three rounds of the medium-dark purple print.

4. Hook three rounds of the light purple print.

5. Hook the remaining center section with the medium-dark purple print.

6. Overcast stitch the outer edge of the canvas.

7. Tie off all loose tails.

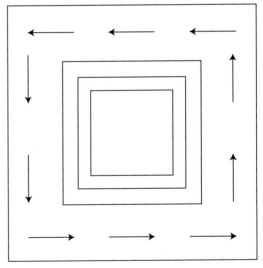

Baby Trivet Construction Diagram

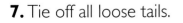

Papa Trivet

Finished size: 12" x 12" (45 x 45 grid).

Supplies

13" x 13" rug canvas

Cotton locker hooking twine

¾ yd. dark brown or rust print

1½ yd. various light and medium autumn-colored
   prints

Locker hook

Blunt tapestry or needlepoint needle

Needle-nose pliers, optional

General tools and supplies

Cut

From	Size	How Many	For
Dark brown or rust print	1½"-wide strips, or your preferred width	As many as yardage allows	Perimeter
Light and medium autumn-colored prints	1½"-wide strips, or your preferred width	As many as yardage allows	Inner rows

Construct

1. Fold the raw edge of the canvas under three rows, overlapping and aligning openings.

2. Hook three or four rounds of dark brown print around the perimeter of the rug canvas; use a circular pattern. Mix and match fabrics, or repeat a single fabric. Refer to the Papa Trivet Construction Diagram.

3. Fill the remaining center with light and medium autumn-colored strips in random order. Hook the rows in a straight line, back and forth, back and forth, left to right, right to left. Use random-length strips to achieve a more pleasing look.

4. Overcast stitch the outer edge of the canvas.

5. Tie off all of the loose tails.

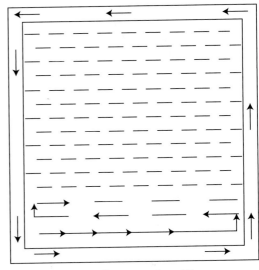

Papa Trivet Construction Diagram

Auntie Mat

Finished size: 11" x 15" (41 x 57 grid).

Supplies

12" × 16" rug canvas

Cotton locker hooking twine

2 yd. medium red/green/purple print

2/3 yd. light green/purple print

1 yd. dark red solid or near solid

½ yd. dark purple solid or near solid

Locker hook

Blunt tapestry or needlepoint needle

Needle-nose pliers, optional

General tools and supplies

Cut

From	Size	How Many	For
Dark red solid	1½"-wide strips, or your preferred width	As many as yardage allows	Perimeter, corner squares
Medium print	1½"-wide strips, or your preferred width	As many as yardage allows	Inner rows
Light print	1½"-wide strips, or your preferred width	As many as yardage allows	Inner rows
Dark purple solid	1½"-wide strips, or your preferred width	As many as yardage allows	Inner rows, center

Construct

1. Fold the raw edge of the canvas under three rows, overlapping and aligning the openings.

2. Hook two rounds of dark red solid around perimeter of rug canvas in a circular pattern. Refer to the Auntie Mat Construction Diagram.

3. Hook dark red solid corner squares, stitching horizontally on each; hook six rows of six stitches in each corner.

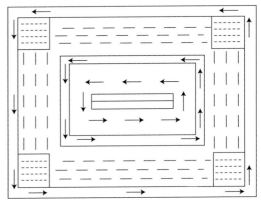

Auntie Mat Construction Diagram

4. Hook nine rows of medium print, beginning near outer edge on a 15" side. Hook in a back-and-forth pattern, parallel to each side; refer to the Auntie Mat Construction Diagram. You'll need to start and stop more than once; the tails will be anchored and hidden later.

5. Hook two rounds of dark purple solid in a circular pattern.

6. Hook four or five rounds light print, depending on the exact amount of grid in your piece. Hook less than half the remaining empty area.

7. Hook one round of medium print (or continue with the light print).

8. Hook the remaining center with dark purple solid.

9. Overcast stitch the outer edge of canvas.

10. Tie off all of the loose tails.

Finished size: 11" x 15" (41 x 57 grid).

Supplies

12" x 16" rug canvas

Cotton locker hooking twine

1⅔ yd. various dark blue solids or near solids

1⅛ yd. medium blue print

⅓ yd. yellow solid or print

¾ yd. light green/yellow/blue print

Locker hook

Blunt tapestry or needlepoint needle

Needle-nose pliers, optional

General tools and supplies

Cut

From	Size	How Many	For
Dark blue solids	1½"-wide strips, or your preferred width	As many as yardage allows	Perimeter
Medium blue print	1½"-wide strips, or your preferred width	As many as yardage allows	Inner rows
Yellow solid or print	1½"-wide strips, or your preferred width	As many as yardage allows	Inner rows
Light print	1½"-wide strips, or your preferred width	As many as yardage allows	Inner rows, center

Construct

1. Fold the raw edge of the canvas under three rows, overlapping and aligning the openings.

2. Hook two rounds of dark blue solids around the perimeter of the rug canvas; use a circular pattern. Begin three holes from a corner on a long side. Refer to the Uncle Mat Construction Diagram.

3. Hook eight rows of dark blue solids on each short side; use a back-and-forth pattern. You will be able to continue hooking from your perimeter rounds on one side, but you will need to start a new strip on the other side.

4. Hook nine rows of medium blue print in a back-and-forth pattern, beginning on one long side.

Uncle Mat Construction Diagram

5. Hook one row of yellow.

6. Hook three rows of light print.

7. Hook one row of yellow.

8. Hook six rows of light print; this is the center area and the design repeats after this section. Count out the exact number of rows you have left and determine the exact number of rows left for this center. It will be approximately six rows. Optional: Start the pattern again on the opposite side of project and fill the center in last.

9. Hook one row of yellow.

10. Hook three rows of light print.

11. Hook one row of yellow.

12. Hook nine rows of medium blue print.

13. Overcast stitch the outer edge of the canvas.

14. Tie off all of the loose tails.

Guest Mat

Finished size: 12" × 18" (45 × 68 grid).

Shown with Lidded Photo Keeper.

Supplies

13" × 19" rug canvas

Cotton locker hooking twine

1¼ yd. dark rust solid or near solid

½ yd. two different dark brown solids or near
  solids, brown 1 and brown 2*

¼ yd. two more dark brown solids or near solids,
  brown 3 and brown 4*

2¼ yd. medium rust/cream/brown print

Locker hook

Blunt tapestry or needlepoint needle

Needle-nose pliers, optional

General tools and supplies

*Note: Four different dark brown fabrics were used.
If you prefer, use 1½ yd. of a single fabric instead.

Cut

From	Size	How Many	For
Dark rust solid	1½"-wide strips, or your preferred width	As many as yardage allows	Perimeter
Dark brown solids 1 and 2	1½"-wide strips, or your preferred width	As many as yardage allows	Rows on the long sides of the mat
Dark brown solids 3 and 4	1½"-wide strips, or your preferred width	As many as yardage allows	Rows on the short sides of the mat
Medium rust print	1½"-wide strips, or your preferred width	As many as yardage allows	Inner rows, center

Construct

1. Fold the raw edge of the canvas under three
rows, overlapping and aligning openings.

2. Hook three rounds of dark rust around the
perimeter of the rug canvas; use a circular pattern.
Begin on a long side and four holes from a corner;
it doesn't matter which corner. Refer to the Guest
Mat Construction Diagram.

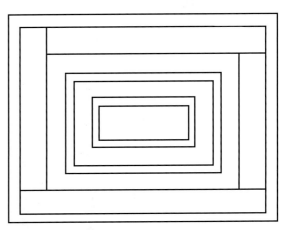

Guest Mat Construction Diagram

3. Hook five rows of dark brown in a back-and-
forth pattern along one 18" side. Or, if you are
using a single brown fabric, hook five rounds in a
circular pattern and skip to Step 6.

4. Turn the piece; hook five rows of dark brown in
a back-and-forth pattern along one 12" side.

5. Repeat for the remaining two sides.

6. Hook four rounds of medium rust print in a circular pattern.

7. Hook one round of dark brown.

8. Hook four rounds of medium print.

9. Hook one round of dark brown.

10. Hook the remaining center area with medium print.

11. Overcast stitch the outer edges of the canvas.

12. Tie off all of the loose tails.

Finished size: 12" × 36" (45 × 135 grid).

Supplies

13" x 37" rug canvas

Cotton locker hooking twine

3 yd. various dark green solids or near solids

6½ yd. various medium pink floral prints

Locker hook

Blunt tapestry or needlepoint needle

Needle-nose pliers, optional

General tools and supplies

Cut

From	Size	How Many	For
Dark green solids	1½"-wide strips, or your preferred width	As many as yardage allows	Perimeter, center frames
Medium pink floral prints	1½"-wide strips, or your preferred width	As many as yardage allows	Inner rows, centers

Construct

1. Fold the raw edge of the canvas under three or four rows, overlapping and aligning openings.

2. Hook three rounds of dark green around the perimeter of rug canvas; use a circular pattern. Mix and match fabrics. Refer to the Neighbor Runner Construction Diagram.

3. Hook six rounds of pink in a circular pattern.

4. Hook two rounds of the dark green frame at one end; you will be stitching next to your pink fabric on three sides. The frame will be 20 stitches or grids along the narrow sides, and approximately 30 stitches or grids along the long sides.

5. Repeat this dark green frame at the other end of your canvas.

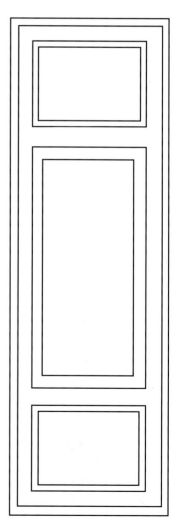

Neighbor Runner Construction Diagram

6. Hook two rounds of dark green frame in the center, leaving a six grid space between this frame and the two end frames.

7. Inside the two outer green frames, hook three rounds of pink, then one round of dark green. Fill the remaining area with pink. Hook in a circular pattern.

8. Inside the center green frame, hook three rounds of pink and two rounds of dark green. Fill the remaining area with pink. Hook in a circular pattern.

9. Hook six rows of pink in the area between the frames; hook this in a back-and-forth pattern in the direction shown. Refer to the Neighbor Runner Construction Diagram.

10. Overcast stitch the outer edge of the canvas.

11. Tie off all of the loose tails.

Family Rug

Finished size: 19" × 28" (71 × 105 grid).

Supplies

20" × 29" rug canvas
Cotton locker hooking twine
3 yd. dark green solid or near solid
8 yd. assorted multicolored pink prints
Locker hook
Blunt tapestry or needlepoint needle
Needle-nose pliers, optional
General tools and supplies

*Note: This project is more difficult and time-consuming than the trivets and mats in this book.

Cut

From	Size	How Many	For
Dark green solid	1½"-wide strips, or your preferred width	As many as yardage allows	Perimeter, center frames
Multicolored pink prints	1½"-wide strips, or your preferred width	As many as yardage allows	Inner rows, center

Construct

1. Fold the raw edge of the canvas under four rows, overlapping and aligning openings.

2. Hook three rounds of dark green around the perimeter of the rug canvas in a circular pattern. Use one fabric, or mix and match prints if you prefer. Refer to the Family Rug Construction Diagram.

3. Count 15 rows from the inner green perimeter on a short side; hook three rows of dark green. Repeat, measuring from the opposite short side. Refer to the Family Rug Construction Diagram and photo for placement of these rows. It's not critical that the spacing between these green "frames" be exactly 15 grids, just that the same spacing is used on the right and left sides of your project.

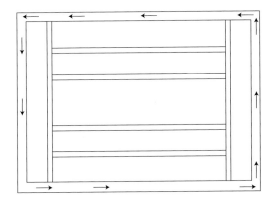

Family Rug Construction Diagram

4. Count 15 rows from the inner green perimeter on a long side; hook a single row of dark green. Count another seven rows toward the center, and hook another single row of dark green. Repeat, measuring from the opposite side of the rug. These are the "framing" rows of dark green. It's not critical that the spacing between these green "frames" be exactly 15 and seven, just that the same spacing is used on each side of your project.

5. Hook the remaining open areas with an assortment of coordinating fabrics, like the various pink and green prints that I have used.

6. Overcast stitch the outer edge of the canvas.

7. Tie off all of the loose tails.

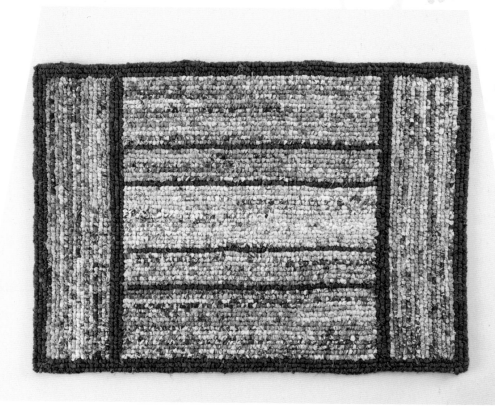

CHAPTER 3

Boxes

This chapter is full of boxes and containers of all sizes and shapes that are ready to hold your special treasures. Begin by reviewing the tips for all containers and the specific tips for boxes. Next, learn the basic construction directions; you'll want to keep that section handy and refer to it often as you make the boxes. The sky is the limit as you sew these boxes, so let your imagination go wild!

Tips for All Containers

- Use a rotary cutter to do as much cutting as possible on your container projects; this will keep your edges clean and keep loose threads to a minimum.
- Protect your ironing board from fusible "accidents." Place a nonstick pressing sheet on the ironing board, and iron on top of it.
- When ironing fabric to stiff interfacing, work from the center outward to avoid creases and bubbles.
- Use smooth yarns or even the cotton twine used in locker hooking projects as cording for these container projects. Avoid fuzzy yarns and threads.
- Use light-colored cording when you stitch with light thread and dark-colored cording with dark thread. The exact color doesn't matter as much as the value (how light or dark) of the color.
- Make it easier to attach cording by using specialty feet. Check your owner's manual or talk to your dealer to find out what presser feet will work with your machine.
- Test your stitch length and width to find the perfect satin stitch settings for your machine. Sew on a scrap of stiff interfacing to obtain the best comparison. Once you find the perfect settings for your machine, write them down for future reference. Refer to the Machine Settings Table on page 66 for suggested settings.
- If you're unhappy with the appearance of your satin stitching after one round of stitching, you can usually correct the problem with a second round sewn a bit wider and tighter.
- Wash the containers following the recommended settings for the fabrics used within each project.
- Re-shape containers after sewing or washing. Use a heat- and steam-resistant shape, such as a dressmaker's ham, wooden block or baking pan, and set your iron to a steam setting. Let the item cool completely before moving it to allow the shape to hold.

Tips for Boxes

- Use a zigzag or satin stitch to sew the box sides together with seams that show on the outside (Lidded Pen Organizer) or with those that are hidden inside (In Boxes).
- Containers with satin-stitched side seams may look complicated, but they are very simple to sew.
- Add cording to the outer edge of your flat box before sewing the side seams. Some of this cording may be trimmed away in the finishing process.
- Leave the excess fabric from sewing side seams inside a box in place. Work them into box designs, or use pinking shears to trim the fabric to a narrower seam allowance.
- Remember: Most boxes are not reversible. There is so much stress put on the seams when the box is turned inside out that they may rip out.
- To make a box a specific size, determine the exact size and shape you need. Make a three-dimensional sketch of your box. Assign measurements to each side — height, width and depth — so you can determine the sizes of the pieces needed. Now, take your diagram and "explode" it so the box lies flat to create a construction diagram. Remember that tall, skinny boxes should be sewn with outside seams, because inside seams may rip out when turned right side out. To design a lid to fit your box, add ¼" to the box measurements. For example, a box that has a 2" x 4" opening will need a lid that is 2¼" x 4¼". The lid should overlap the box half the height or less (or fit according to your preference).

Box Construction

1. Cut the pieces as listed. For template pieces, copy the shape onto scrap paper, card stock or template plastic, and cut it out. Trace around this template, and cut the pieces as listed.

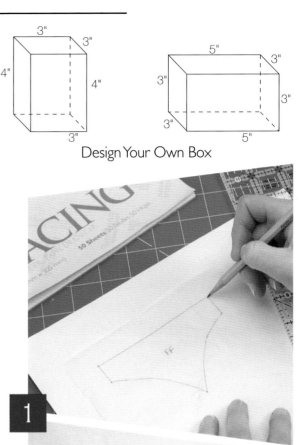

Design Your Own Box

2. Iron fusible web to the wrong side of all of the fabric pieces, unless specified otherwise. Follow the manufacturer's directions. Remove all of the paper backing. Disregard this step if your stiff interfacing already has fusible web on both sides of it, or if you prefer to use a glue stick or temporary spray adhesive instead of fusible web.

3. Refer to the construction diagram(s) for your project, and arrange the interfacing pieces as indicated.

4. Use white thread to stitch the interfacing pieces together as marked on the diagram; follow Steps 5 through 7 if you are sewing the interfacing as one large unit (recommended for large projects). Complete Step 8 if you are sewing it as separate pieces (recommended for small pieces). Sew with a wide and long zigzag stitch; refer to the Machine Settings Table on page 66 for suggested settings.

Note: The fabrics shown on pages 61-71 were provided by P&B Textiles. The decorative threads shown on pages 63-71 were provided by Sulky of America.

5. To sew the interfacing as one large unit, cut the interfacing pieces listed for your project. Position them as shown in the construction diagram.

6. Sew the pieces together where they touch (shown as a zigzag line in the diagram). Keep the pieces slightly apart as you sew with a loose zigzag stitch (suggested settings: length = 2, width = 4). If the pieces are butted up to each other tightly, it's hard to get a crisp edge on your box.

7. Iron the fabric to the interfacing, or use a glue stick or temporary spray adhesive. Proceed to Step 9.

8. To sew the interfacing as separate units, cut the interfacing pieces listed for your project. Position them on the wrong side of your container fabric as shown in your construction diagram; leave about 1/16" of space between pieces. Tack the pieces in place with a glue stick.

9. Trim the piece as shown in the trimming diagram. Repeat this process with the lining fabric on the other side of interfacing; again trim fabric as shown in diagram. Note: For inside seams, usually you'll trim the shape to a square or a rectangle. For outside seams, generally trim the piece to the exact shape of the interfacing.

10. Quilt the piece as desired. Trim all of the threads.

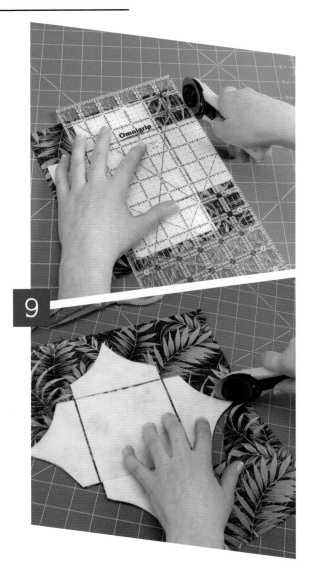

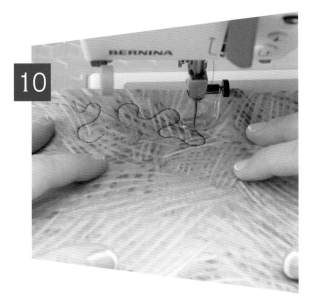

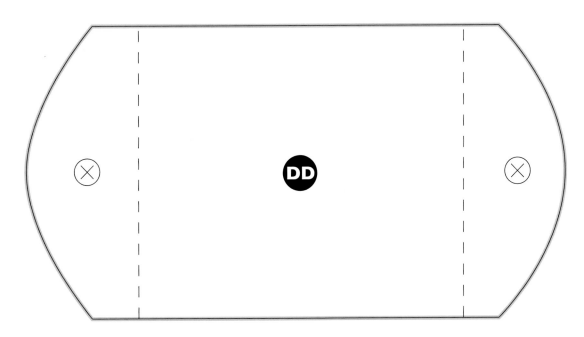

Flip Top Box – Lid Template DD

11. Work from the right side of your project. Refer to the green line on the trimming and cording diagram(s) for your project to see exactly where cording should be added. Refer to the Machine Settings Table on page 66 for suggested settings.

12. Sew with a satin stitch over the cording to finish the outer edges. Use a cording foot (optional) and zigzag stitch over the cording; use a thread to match or contrast the fabric as you prefer. Refer to the Machine Settings Table on page 66 for suggested machine settings.

13. Repeat the zigzag stitch if the first stitching does not completely cover the cording and raw edge; sew with a tighter and wider stitch. You will be sewing over the previous stitching with no cording this time. This tight zigzag stitch is also called a satin stitch, and it gives finished edges a professional look. Refer to the Machine Settings Table for suggested machine settings.

14. To create boxes and lids where the side seams are on the outside, proceed to Steps 17 through 19.

Outside seams.

15. To create boxes and lids where the side seams are on the inside, proceed to Steps 20 through 22.

16. To finish the flaps for inside seams, proceed to Steps 23 through 26.

Inside seams.

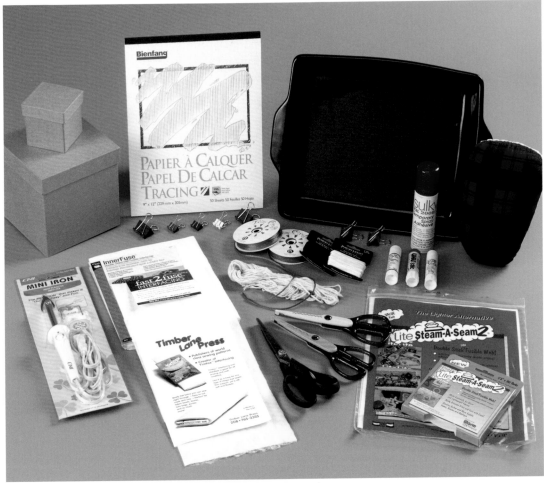

Box making tools.

MACHINE SETTINGS TABLE

Suggested Starting Zigzag Settings

Use these settings as a starting point to determine the best zigzag stitch needed for your machine and fabrics. Make a test piece using the same materials to find the perfect settings for your machine. If one round of stitching covers nicely, skip the second round.

1. Sew interfacing pieces together:
  Stitch length = 2
  Stitch width = 4

2. First round of zigzag stitching (often over cording):
  Stitch length = ⅜
  Stitch width = 3¾ to 4

3. Second round of zigzag stitching:
  Stitch length = Less than ⅜
  Stitch width = 4¼

Your Machine's Best Zigzag Settings

As you complete some test stitching and tweak your machine's settings, it will become clear what zigzag stitch lengths and widths work the best. Jot down that information below for your handy reference.

Date: _____ Your Machine Type:_____

Interfacing

  Stitch length: _____

  Stitch width: _____

First round zigzag stitching

  Stitch length: _____

  Stitch width: _____

Second round zigzag stitching

  Stitch length: _____

  Stitch width: _____

OUTSIDE SEAMS

17. To sew the side seams of a box or lid with the seams on the outside, fold the box so it is right side out, as if it is already finished. Choose one corner; squish the box flat as you align the upper edges and sides at that corner. If desired, hold it together with binder clips. Don't be shy! You will re-shape this later.

18. Begin at the upper edge of the corner, and sew with a zigzag stitch; stop ⅛" before the box bottom. Backstitch at the beginning and the end of the stitching; use the same stitch width as your original zigzag stitch and a stitch length of ½. Test these settings to find what is best for your fabric and your machine.

TIP

Use a cording foot on the box projects; this presser foot is designed to simplify sewing with cording or thick yarn. Cording feeds through a hole in the foot, and grooves guide it under the needle consistently in the same position. Why add cording to your project in the first place? The edges finish nicer with cording, and it usually takes less thread for coverage.

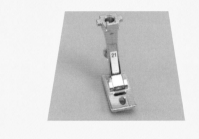

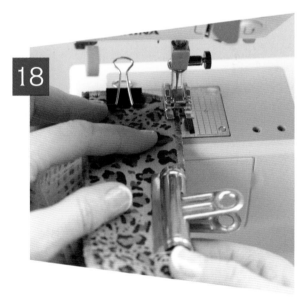

19. For an optional method often used with lids, fold the lid right side out along the intersections of stiff interfacing, as if it were already finished and ready to put on your box. The raw edges are already satin stitched and finished. Simply tack the lower edges of the sides together at each corner by hand. Proceed to Step 27.

INSIDE SEAMS

20. To sew the side seams of a box or lid with the seams on the inside, fold the box so it is wrong side out. Choose one corner, and squish the box flat with right sides together as you align the upper edges and sides at that one corner; feel for the layers of stiff interfacing. Crease, mark or pin this seam line as needed. An extra flap of fabric will extend to the side with its upper edges aligned.

21. Begin at the upper edge, and sew alongside the interfacing; stop ⅛" from the box bottom. Sew with a straight stitch (suggested length = 2), and backstitch well at the beginning and end. The upper part of your seams will be stressed when the box is turned right side out. Backstitch well near the upper edge to reinforce this seam. Repeat for all of the box sides.

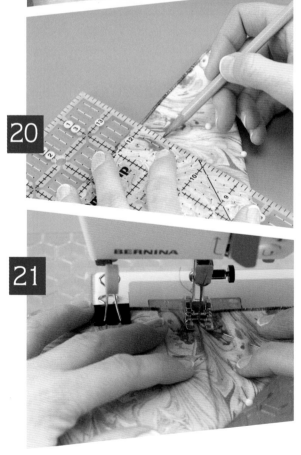

22. Turn the box or lid right side out. Take care of the excess flap of fabric at each corner, using one of the following options as you prefer. Then, proceed to Step 27.

23. To pink the edges, begin with the box or lid wrong side out. Use pinking shears to trim away the excess flap at each corner; leave a ¼" to ⅜" seam allowance. Cut the upper edge at a slight angle.

24. To finish the edges using the pleat and wrap method, begin with the box or lid right side out. Pleat the excess fabric at each corner as you would pleat the corners of a long dining room tablecloth. Wrap the tip of this fabric up and over the box corner, centering it over the side seam on the right side of the box. Tack the fabric in place at the tip by hand or machine.

25. For the pleat and trim edge finish, begin with the box or lid right side out. Pleat the excess fabric as for the pleat and wrap option. Baste it in place at the upper edge with a long straight stitch sewn just below your satin stitching. Trim off the points that extend beyond the box. Finish the raw edges with a satin stitch and optional cording.

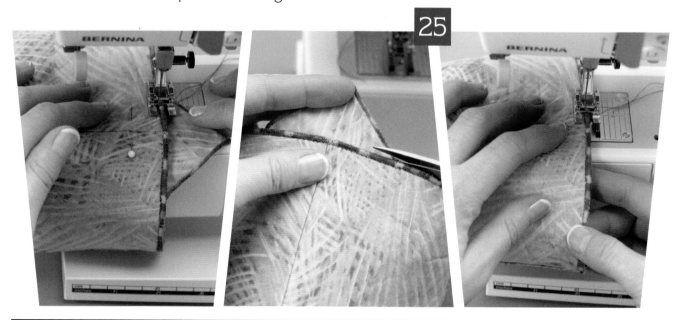

26. For the fold and tack finish, leave the flaps intact. Fold a flap to the side of the box, and tack it in place by hand at each point. Very small flaps need no tacking and can be left "unfinished."

27. Re-shape the box and lid. Steam iron the piece while it is supported by a heat- and steam-resistant shape, such as a dressmaker's shape, a wooden block or a baking pan. Let the item cool completely before moving it. Some boxes can be re-shaped by folding them up like purchased gift boxes and then pressing them flat from both sides. Let the box cool in position before moving it or opening it up. For quick touch-ups, crease each seam by hand, like you would in cardmaking.

Four Cubed Tassel Box

Finished size: 4" x 4" x 4".

This lidded box features a fancy lid design and tassel trim.

Supplies

⅜ yd. stripe (box, lid lining)

⅜ yd. floral print (box lining, lid)

2 skeins yellow 6-strand embroidery floss

4½" x 4½" tracing paper, scrap paper or template plastic

Fine-tooth comb

Embroidery needle

⅓ yd. Fast2Fuse, 28" wide, or ⅓ yd. Timtex, 22" wide, plus 1½ yd. lightweight fusible web, 16" wide

3 yd. cording, 1/16" diameter

Thread

Glue stick (optional)

Temporary spray adhesive (optional)

Cording foot for machine (optional)

Heat- and steam-resistant shape (optional)

General tools and supplies listed in Chapter 1

Note: If you are using a stiff interfacing with fusible web already on both sides of it, omit the fusible web in the supplies and cutting instructions. Disregard the reference to fusible web in the construction steps. A glue stick or temporary spray adhesive may be used in place of the fusible web.

Cut

From	Size	How Many	For
Stripe	13" x 13" 11" x 11"	1 1	Box, B Lid lining, E
Floral print	13" x 13" 11" x 11"	1 1	Box lining, B Lid, E
Stiff interfacing	4" x 4" 4¼" x 4¼" Template FF	5 1 4	Box bottom and sides, A Lid top, C Lid sides, FF
Fusible web	13" x 13" 11" x 11"	2 2	Box, B Lid lining, E

Construct

1. Follow the general Box Construction steps and the inside seam directions to create the box.

2. Follow the pleat and wrap finish treatment instructions.

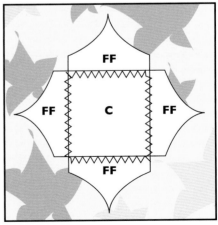

Four Cubed Tassel Box – Lid Construction Diagram

3. Create the lid following the outside seam instructions. Use Template FF for the lid sides, and tack them at the lower edge following the optional method.

4. Use yellow embroidery floss to create four 1½" tassels. Refer to Chapter 1 for detailed instructions. Attach the tassels by hand or machine to the points of the lid.

5. Re-shape the box and lid.

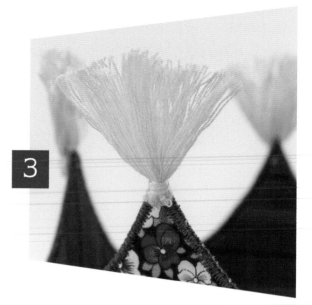

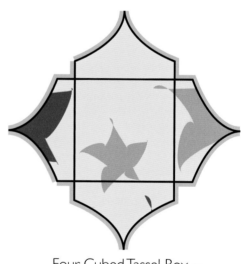

Four Cubed Tassel Box –
Lid Trimming & Cording Diagram

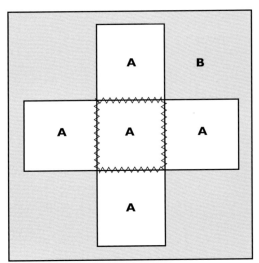

Four Cubed Tassel Box –
Box Construction Diagram

Four Cubed Tassel Box –
Box Trimming & Cording Diagram

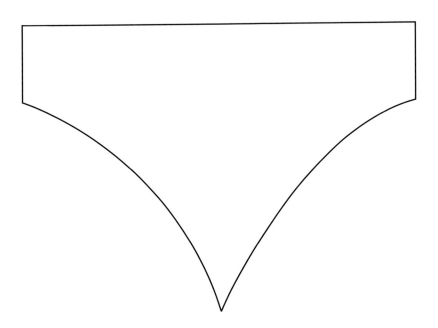

Four Cubed Tassel Box – Lid Template FF

Finished size: 4" × 4" × 4".

This variation features a traditional lid with the
fabric flap pleated and wrapped to the front. Fabrics provided by
P&B Textiles, and decorative thread provided by Sulky of America.

Supplies

½ yd. safari print (box, lid, lid lining)

1 fat quarter coordinating print (box lining)

⅓ yd. Fast2Fuse, 28" wide, or ⅓ yd. Timtex,
    22" wide, plus 1½ yd. lightweight fusible web,
    16" wide

3 yd. cording, ¹⁄₁₆" diameter

Thread

Glue stick (optional)

Temporary spray adhesive (optional)

Cording foot for machine (optional)

Heat- and steam-resistant shape (optional)

General tools and supplies listed in Chapter 1

Note: If you are using a stiff interfacing with fusible web already on both sides of it, omit the fusible web in the supplies and cutting instructions. Disregard the reference to fusible web in the construction steps. A glue stick or temporary spray adhesive may be used in place of the fusible web.

Cut

From	Size	How Many	For
Safari print	13" x 13" 11" x 11"	1 2	Box, B Lid; lid lining, E
Coordinating print	13" x 13"	1	Box lining, B
Stiff interfacing	4" x 4" 4¼" x 4¼" 1¾" x 4¼"	5 1 4	Box bottom and sides, A Lid top, C Lid sides, D
Fusible web	13" x 13" 11" x 11"	2 2	Box, B Lid, E

Construct

1. Follow the general Box Construction steps and the inside seam directions to create the box and lid. Refer to the Four Cubed Tassel Box Construction Diagram and Trimming and Cording Diagram. For the lid, refer to the CD Keeper Lid Trimming and Cording Diagram.

2. Follow the pleat and wrap directions to finish the flaps on both the box and lid.

3. Re-shape the box and lid.

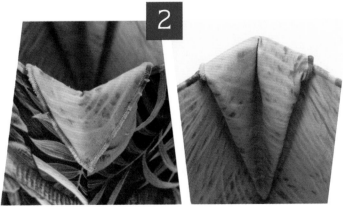

Variation: Four Cubed Valentine Box

Finished size: 4" × 4" × 4".

This variation features a different lid design and button trim.

Supplies

⅜ yd. print 1 (box, lid lining)

⅜ yd. print 2 (box lining, lid)

⅓ yd. Fast2Fuse, 28" wide, or ⅓ yd. Timtex, 22" wide, plus 1½ yd. lightweight fusible web, 16" wide

3 yd. cording, ¹⁄₁₆" diameter

4½" × 4½" tracing paper, scrap paper or template plastic

4 buttons, ⅜" diameter

Thread

Glue stick (optional)

Temporary spray adhesive (optional)

Cording foot for machine (optional)

Heat- and steam-resistant shape (optional)

General tools and supplies listed in Chapter 1

Note: If you are using a stiff interfacing with fusible web already on both sides of it, omit the fusible web in the supplies and cutting instructions. Disregard the reference to fusible web in the construction steps. A glue stick or temporary spray adhesive may be used in place of the fusible web.

Cut

From	Size	How Many	For
Print 1	13" x 13" 11" x 11"	1 1	Box, B Lid lining, E
Print 2	13" x 13" 11" x 11"	1 1	Box lining, B Lid, E
Stiff interfacing	4" x 4" 4¼" x 4¼" Template GG	5 1 4	Box bottom and sides, A Lid top, C Lid sides, GG
Fusible web	13" x 13" 11" x 11"	2 2	Box, B Lid, E

Construct

1. Follow the general Box Construction steps and the directions for inside seams to construct the box; finish the flaps with the pleat and trim method. Refer to the box diagrams for the Four Cubed Tassel Box.

2. Follow the general Box Construction steps and directions for inside seams to create the lid; use Template GG for the lid sides. Finish the inside seam flaps with the fold and tack technique (or do nothing at all).

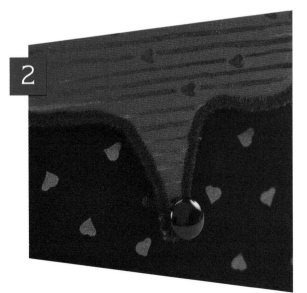

3. Sew one button by hand to each point on the lid.

4. Re-shape the box and lid.

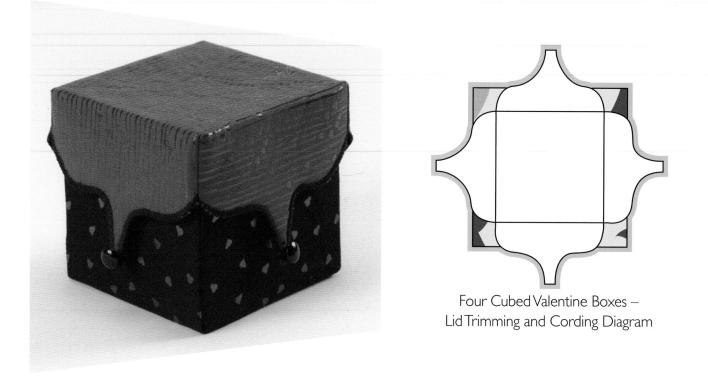

Four Cubed Valentine Boxes –
Lid Trimming and Cording Diagram

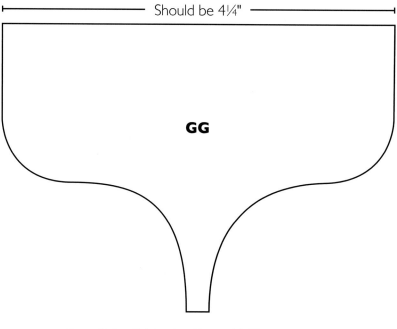

Should be 4¼"

GG

Four Cubed Valentine Box - Lid Template GG

Finished size: 4½" × 6½" × 2½".
This box, shown with the Guest Mat, features a clear
pocket on the lid to show off a special picture. It is constructed with inside seams.

Supplies

1 fat quarter print (box, lid)

1 fat quarter solid (box lining, lid lining)

¼ yd. Fast2Fuse, 28" wide, or ¼ yd. Timtex,
22" wide plus 1¼ yd. lightweight fusible web,
16" wide

3 yd. cording, ⅟₁₆" diameter

4" x 6" clear vinyl

Thread

Glue stick (optional)

Temporary spray adhesive (optional)

Cording foot for machine (optional)

Heat- and steam-resistant shape (optional)

General tools and supplies listed in Chapter 1

Note: If you are using a stiff interfacing with fusible web already on both sides of it, omit the fusible web in the supplies and cutting instructions. Disregard the reference to fusible web in the construction steps. A glue stick or temporary spray adhesive may be used in place of the fusible web.

Cut

From	Size	How Many	For
Print	10½" x 12½" 8" x 10"	1 1	Box, D Lid, H
Solid	10½" x 12½" 8" x 10"	1 1	Box lining, D Lid lining, H
Vinyl	3½" x 5½"	1	Pocket
Stiff interfacing	4½" x 6½" 2½" x 4½" 2½" x 6½" 4¾" x 6¾" 1" x 4¾" 1" x 6¾"	1 2 2 1 2 2	Box bottom, A Box sides, B Box sides, C Lid top, E Lid sides, F Lid sides, G
Fusible web	10½" x 12½" 8" x 10"	2 2	Box, D Lid, H

Construct

1. Follow the general Box Construction steps and the directions for inside seams to construct the box. Refer to the construction diagrams and Trimming and Cording Diagrams for the In Boxes.

2. Pink the edges of the inside seams to finish them.

3. Create the lid following the general construction steps and inside seam directions. Refer to the diagrams for the In Boxes. Before sewing the side seams, proceed to the next step.

4. Center the vinyl piece on top of the lid. Sew the pocket to the lid on three sides using a wide and long zigzag stitch (suggested settings: length = 2, width = 4). Backstitch at the beginning and end. If the zigzag stitching is too tight, it will cut through the vinyl.

5. Complete the lid.

6. Pink the edges of the lid's inside seams to finish them.

7. Re-shape the box and lid. Be careful to keep the iron away from the vinyl.

Flip Top Box

Finished size: 2" x 4" x 4".

This box, shown with braided coasters that measure

roughly 3" in diameter, features a flip top lid. It is constructed with inside seams.

Supplies

1 fat quarter print (box, lid)

1 fat quarter solid (box lining, lid lining)

¼ yd. Fast2Fuse, 28" wide, or ¼ yd. Timtex, 22" wide, plus ¾ yd. lightweight fusible web, 16" wide

3½ yd. cording, ¹⁄₁₆" diameter

3½" x 6½" tracing paper, scrap paper, cardstock or template plastic

Marking pencil suitable for your fabrics, such as a chalk pencil or standard pencil

1 hook and loop tape dot, ½" in diameter or 1 medium snap

2 buttons, ¾" diameter

Thread

Glue stick (optional)

Temporary spray adhesive (optional)

Cording foot for machine (optional)

Heat- and steam-resistant shape (optional)

General tools and supplies listed in Chapter 1

Note: If you are using a stiff interfacing with fusible web already on both sides of it, omit the fusible web in the supplies and cutting instructions. Disregard the reference to fusible web in the construction steps. A glue stick or temporary spray adhesive may be used in place of the fusible web.

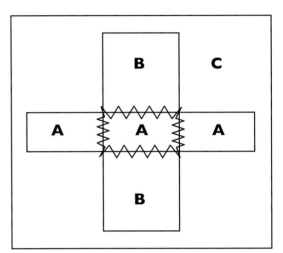

Flip Top Box – Box Construction Diagram

Cut

From	Size	How Many	For
Print	11" x 13" DD Template	1 1	Box, C Lid, DD
Solid	11" x 13" DD Template	1 1	Box lining, C Lid lining, DD
Stiff interfacing	2" x 4" 4" x 4" DD Template	3 2 1	Box bottom and sides, A Box sides, B Lid, DD
Fusible web	11" x 13" DD Template	2 2	Box, C Lid, DD

Construct

1. Follow the general Box Construction steps and the directions for inside seams.

2. Pink the box seams to finish them.

3. Follow the general construction steps to complete the lid; use Template DD on page 63.

4. Mark "X" points on the right side of the lid pieces as shown on the DD template. Use a marking tool that shows up but is removable, like a chalk pencil. These points are placement guides for the buttons and hook-and-loop tape closure.

5. Place the lid (DD) on the box as in the finished sample, overlapping one edge so the dashed line is at the top of the box.

6. Sew one button by hand at the "X," sewing through the button, the lid and the box. Make a knot at the beginning and the end of your stitching. This is the backside of your box.

7. On the lining side of the other end of the lid, sew one hook-and-loop-tape dot or snap at the "X." Sew a button in the same place, but on the right side of the fabric. This will hide the previous stitches and make it look like you have a button closure.

8. Pull the lid to the front of the box, overlapping the dashed line. Mark where the other half of the hook-and-loop or snap closure should be sewn to the box. Sew the second half of the hook-and-loop tape or snap at this point by hand, sewing only through the closure and box front; make a knot at the beginning and the end of stitching.

9. Re-shape the box.

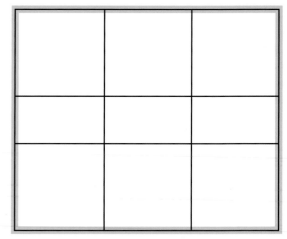

Flip Top Box –
Box Trimming & Cording Diagram

6

TIP

Get extra mileage from your fabric scraps by making a set of coordinating braided coasters. Simply follow the instructions in Chapter 1 for creating braid trim. Coil a length of braid into a circular form, and tack the coils in place.

Square Basket with Braided Trim

Finished size: 7" × 7".
This open box features curved sides and braid trim.
It is constructed with inside seams, and it is the perfect size to hold paper napkins.

Supplies

⅔ yd. print (box, braid)

⅝ yd. solid (box lining, braid)

¼ yd. heavyweight Fast2Fuse, 28" wide,
   or ¼ yd. Timtex, 22" wide, plus 1 yd. lightweight
   fusible web, 16" wide

2 yd. cording, ¹⁄₁₆" diameter

Thread

4" × 8" tracing paper, scrap paper, card stock or
   template plastic

Small clamp, office clips, safety pins,
   rubber bands (braid)

Glue stick (optional)

Temporary spray adhesive (optional)

Cording foot for machine (optional)

Heat- and steam-resistant shape (optional)

General tools and supplies listed in Chapter 1

Note: If you are using a stiff interfacing with fusible web already on both sides of it, omit the fusible web in the supplies and cutting instructions. Disregard the reference to fusible web in the construction steps. A glue stick or temporary adhesive may be used in place of the fusible web.

Cut

From	Size	How Many	For
Print	2"-wide strips	4	Braid
	15" x 15"	1	Box, D
Solid	2"-wide strips	2	Braid
	15" x 15"	1	Box lining, D
Stiff interfacing	7" x 7"	1	Box bottom, A
	3¼" x 7"	2	Box sides, B
	Template CC	2	Curved box sides, CC
Fusible web	15" x 15"	2	Box, D

Construct

1. Follow the general Box Construction steps and the directions for inside seams.

2. Pink the seam edges to finish them.

3. Make the braid trim using 2"-wide strips; refer to Chapter 1 for detailed instructions. Sew two print strips together along the 2" side after removing the selvages; repeat with the other pair of print

3

strips and the pair of solid strips. Make at least 34" of braid.

4. Attach the braid trim to the rim of the box by hand or machine.

5. Re-shape the box.

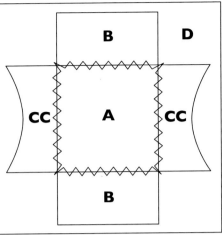

Square Basket – Construction Diagram

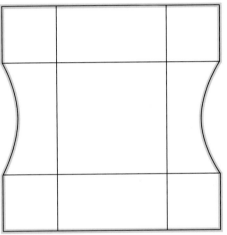

Square Basket – Trimming & Cording Diagram

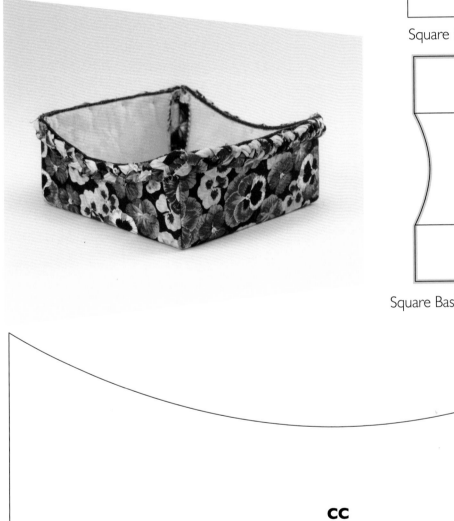

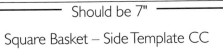

Should be 7"

Square Basket – Side Template CC

Hinged Box

Finished size: 3½" × 3½" × 8½".

This container features a hinged lid.

Supplies

1 fat quarter print 1 (box, lid)

1 fat quarter print 2 (box lining, lid lining)

⅓ yd. heavyweight Fast2Fuse, 28" wide,
  or ½ yd. Timtex, 22" wide, plus 1½ yd.
  lightweight fusible web, 16" wide

3 yd. cording, 1/16" diameter

Thread

15" square ruler

6" x 24" ruler

Marking pencil suitable for your fabrics
  (chalk pencil, standard pencil)

Glue stick (optional)

Temporary spray adhesive (optional)

Cording foot for machine (optional)

Heat- and steam-resistant shape (optional)

General tools and supplies listed in Chapter 1

Note: This project is best made with heavy-weight Fast2Fuse or standard-weight Timtex. If you are using a stiff interfacing with fusible web already on both sides of it, omit the fusible web in the supplies, cutting instructions and construction steps. A glue stick or temporary spray adhesive may be used in place of the fusible web.

Cut

From	Size	How Many	For
Print 1	12" x 17" 7" x 14"	1 1	Box, C Lid, G
Print 2	12" x 17" 7" x 14"	1 1	Box lining, C Lid lining, G
Stiff interfacing	3½" x 8½" 3½" x 3½" 3⅝" x 8⅝" 2" x 8⅝" 2" x 3⅝"	3 2 1 1 2	Box bottom and sides, A Box sides, B Lid top, D Lid side, E Lid sides, F
Fusible web	12" x 17" 7" x 14"	2 2	Box, C Lid, G

Construct

1. Follow the general Box Construction steps and directions for the inside seams to create the box.

2. Pink the edges of the seam allowance to finish them.

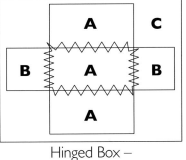

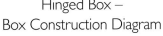

Hinged Box –
Box Construction Diagram

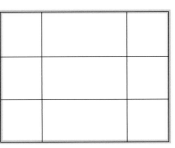

Hinged Box –
Box Trimming &
Cording Diagram

3. Follow the general construction steps and inside seam directions to create the lid, remembering that there are only three sides to be sewn.

4. Pink the lid seams to finish them.

5. Mark the hinge points on the right side of the lid as shown in the diagram. Use a marking tool that shows up on your fabric but is removable.

6. Place the lid on the box top, as if the project were complete; hold the lid in place. Sew lid to box at each hinge point; sew by hand in a wrapping motion with doubled thread (or use a heavier weight thread).

7. Tack the lid securely, but avoid tacking it too tight, or it won't work as a hinge. Make a knot at the beginning and the end of the stitching; hide the knots inside box or lid area. Repeat for each hinge point.

8. Re-shape the box.

Alter your pattern piece sizes and fabric choices to make custom-sized hinged boxes to store all of your stuff. This box, which measures 3½" x 3½" x 12", is the perfect size to store an 11" fashion doll or other toys. To make the ribbon ties for the hinges, sew tiny buttonholes on both the box and the lid at each hinge point. Tie the lid to the box at each hinge point using ⅛"-wide ribbon or yarn.

6

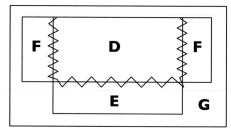

F · D · F

E · G

Hinged Box – Lid Construction Diagram

Hinged Box –
Lid Trimming & Cording Diagram

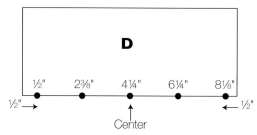

D

½"   2⅜"   4¼"   6¼"   8⅛"

½" → | ← ½"

Center

Hinged Box – Lid Hinge Points

Lidded Wine Box

Finished size: 4½" x 4½" x 14½".
This lidded box provides the perfect way to present a
bottle of wine to your favorite host or hostess. It is constructed with inside seams.

Supplies

½ yd. print 1 (box)

1 yd. print 2 (lid, lid lining, box lining)

⅝ yd. heavyweight Fast2Fuse, 28" wide, or
⅞ yd. Timtex, 22" wide, plus 2¾ yd. lightweight
fusible web, 16" wide

5 yd. cording, 1⁄16" diameter

Thread

Glue stick (optional)

Temporary spray adhesive (optional)

Cording foot for machine (optional)

Heat- and steam-resistant shape (optional)

4 to 5 yd. ribbon, 1½" wide (optional)

General tools and supplies listed in Chapter 1

Note: This project is best made with heavyweight Fast2Fuse or standard-weight Timtex. If you are using a stiff interfacing with fusible web already on both sides of it, omit the fusible web in the supplies and cutting instructions. Disregard the reference to fusible web in the construction steps. A glue stick or temporary spray adhesive may be used in place of the fusible web.

Cut

From	Size	How Many	For
Print 1	15" x 26"	1	Box, C
Print 2	15" x 26"	1	Box lining, C
	10" x 20"	2	Lid, lid lining, G
Stiff interfacing	4½" x 14½"	3	Box bottom and sides, A
	4½" x 4½"	2	Box sides, B
	4¾" x 14¾"	1	Lid top, B
	2" x 14¾"	2	Lid sides, E
	2" x 4¾"	2	Lid sides, F
Fusible web	15" x 26"	2	Box, C
	10" x 20"	2	Lid, G

Construct

1. Follow the general Box Construction steps and the directions for inside seams. Construct the box and lid.

2. Complete the pleat and trim flap technique for the box to finish the inside seams.

3. Pink the flaps of the lid seams to finish them.

4. Re-shape the box and lid.

5. Tie decorative ribbon around the box, and add a bow (optional). Refer to Chapter 1 for bow-making instructions.

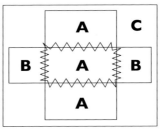

Lidded Wine Box –
Box Construction Diagram

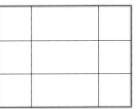

Lidded Wine Box –
Box Trimming
& Cording Diagram

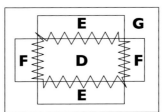

Lidded Wine Box –
Lid Construction Diagram

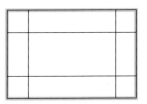

Lidded Wine Box –
Lid Trimming &
Cording Diagram

Finished size: 5¼" × 5¼" × 6".

The lidded CD keeper is constructed with inside seams.

Fabrics provided by P&B Textiles; decorative thread provided by Sulky of America.

Supplies

1 fat quarter print 1 (box)

1 fat quarter print 2 (lid)

½ yd. print 3 (box lining, lid lining)

⅜ yd. heavyweight Fast2Fuse, 28" wide,
 or ½ yd. Timtex, 22" wide plus 1½ yd. lightweight
 fusible web, 16" wide

3½ yd. cording, 1/16" diameter

Thread

Glue stick (optional)

Temporary spray adhesive (optional)

Cording foot for machine (optional)

Heat- and steam-resistant shape (optional)

General tools and supplies listed in Chapter 1

Note: This project is best made with heavy-weight Fast2Fuse or standard-weight Timtex. If you are using a stiff interfacing with fusible web already on both sides of it, omit the fusible web in the supplies and cutting instructions. Disregard the reference to fusible web in the construction steps. A glue stick or temporary spray adhesive may be used in place of the fusible web.

Cut

From	Size	How Many	For
Print 1	18" x 18"	1	Box, C
Print 2	10½" x 10½"	1	Lid, F
Print 3	18" x 18" 10½" x 10½"	1 1	Lid lining, F Box lining, C
Stiff interfacing	5¼" x 5¼" 5¼" x 6" 5½" x 5½" 2" x 5½"	1 4 1 4	Box bottom, A Box sides, B Lid top, D Lid sides, E
Fusible Web	18" x 18" 10½" x 10½"	2 2	Box, C Lid, F

Construct

1. Follow the general Box Construction steps and the directions for inside seams. Construct the box and lid.

2. Pink the flaps of the box seams to finish them.

3. Complete the fold and tack technique to finish the lid flaps.

4. Re-shape the box and lid.

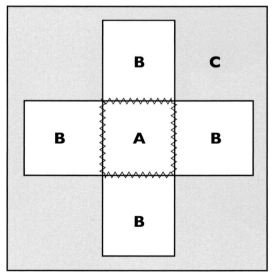

CD Keeper – Box Construction Diagram

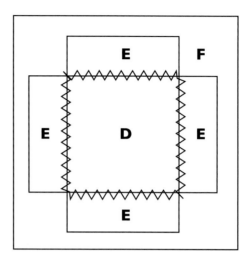

Lidded CD Keeper –
Box Trimming & Cording Diagram

Lidded CD Keeper –
Lid Construction Diagram

TIP

Too many tools and too few drawers? Keep your essentials out of sight but close at hand with the chic boxes featured in this chapter. Mix and match the Lidded CD Keeper, Lidded Square Boxes, Lidded Cube Boxes, Lidded In Boxes, Lidded Pen Organizer and Lidded Organizer projects to create tidy storage solutions for your desk, home office or sewing space. From funky to floral, contemporary to classic, set the tone for the space with the perfect fabrics.

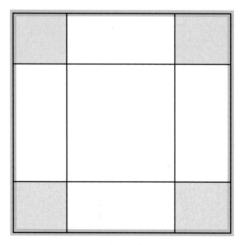

Lidded CD Keeper –
Lid Trimming & Cording Diagram

Lidded Square Boxes

Finished sizes: Small box measures 2½" x 2½" x 1½";

medium box measures 3½" x 3½" x 2"; large measures 4½" x 4½" x 2½".

These nestable boxes feature inside seams and are perfect for fat-quarter bundles of fabric.

Fabrics provided by P&B Textiles; decorative thread provided by Sulky of America.

Supplies (for one box)

Small Box (large scraps may work for this size)

1 fat quarter print 1 (box)
1 fat quarter print 2 (lid)
1 fat quarter print 3 (box lining, lid lining)
¼ yd. Fast2Fuse, 28" wide, or ¼ yd. Timtex,
   22" wide, plus ½ yd. fusible web, 16" wide
1½ yd. cording, ¹⁄₁₆" diameter

Medium Box

1 fat quarter print 1 (box)
1 fat quarter print 2 (lid)
1 fat quarter print 3 (box lining, lid lining)
¼ yd. Fast2Fuse, 28" wide, or ¼ yd. Timtex,
   22" wide, plus ⅝ yd. fusible web, 16" wide
2 yd. cording, ¹⁄₁₆" diameter

Large Box

1 fat quarter print 1 (box)
1 fat quarter print 2 (lid)
1 fat quarter print 3 (box lining, lid lining)
⅓ yd. Fast2Fuse, 28" wide, or ½ yd. Timtex,
   22" wide, plus 1¼ yd. fusible web, 16" wide
2½ yd. cording, ¹⁄₁₆" diameter

Other Supplies

Thread
Glue stick (optional)
Temporary spray adhesive (optional)
Cording foot for sewing machine (optional)
Heat- and steam-resistant shapes (optional)
General tools and supplies listed in Chapter 1

Note: If you are using a stiff interfacing with fusible web already on both sides of it, omit the fusible web in the supplies and cutting instructions. Disregard the reference to fusible web in the construction steps. A glue stick or temporary spray adhesive may be used in place of the fusible web.

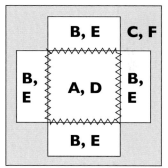

Lidded Square Boxes –
Box and Lid Construction Diagram

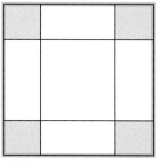

Lidded Square Boxes –
Box and Lid
Trimming & Cording Diagram

Cut

Small Box

From	Size	How Many	For
Print 1	6½" x 6½"	1	Box, C
Print 2	5" x 5"	1	Lid, F
Print 3	6½" x 6½" 5" x 5"	1 1	Box lining, C Lid lining, F
Stiff interfacing	2½" x 2½" 1½" x 2½" 2¾" x 2¾" ¾" x 2¾"	1 4 1 4	Box bottom, A Box sides, B Lid top, D Lid sides, E
Fusible web	6½" x 6½" 5" x 5"	2 2	Box, C Lid, F

Medium Box

From	Size	How Many	For
Print 1	8½" x 8½"	1	Box
Print 2	7" x 7"	1	Lid, F
Print 3	8½" x 8½" 7" x 7"	1 1	Box lining Lid lining
Stiff interfacing	3½" x 3½" 2" x 3½" 3¾" x 3¾" 1" x 3¾"	1 4 1 4	Box bottom Box sides Lid top Lid sides
Fusible web	8½" x 8½" 7" x 7"	2 2	Box Lid

Large Box

From	Size	How Many	For
Print 1	10½" x 10½"	1	Box
Print 2	8½" x 8½"	1	Lid
Print 3	10½" x 10½" 8½" x 8½"	1 1	Box lining Lid lining
Stiff interfacing	4½" x 4½" 2½" x 4½" 4¾" x 4¾" 1½" x 4¾"	1 4 1 4	Box bottom Box sides Lid top Lid sides
Fusible web	10½" x 10½" 8½" x 8½"	2 2	Box Lid

Construct

1. Follow the general Box Construction steps and the inside seam directions to construct the box and lid. Refer to the same trimming and cording diagram.

2. Pink the flaps of all seams to finish them.

3. Re-shape the box and lid.

Lidded Cube Boxes

Finished sizes: Small box measures 2½" x 2½" x 2½"; medium box measures 3½" x 3½" x 3½"; and large box measures 4½" x 4½" x 4½". These nestable cube boxes feature inside seams. Fabrics provided by P&B Textiles; decorative thread provided by Sulky of America.

Supplies (for one box)

Small Box (large scraps may work for this size)

1 fat quarter print 1 (box)

1 fat quarter print 2 (lid)

1 fat quarter print 3 (box lining, lid lining)

¼ yd. Fast2Fuse, 28" wide, or ¼ yd. Timtex,
   22" wide, plus ½ yd. fusible web, 16" wide

2 yd. cording, ¹⁄₁₆" diameter

Medium Box

1 fat quarter print 1 (box)

1 fat quarter print 2 (lid)

1 fat quarter print 3 (box lining, lid lining)

¼ yd. Fast2Fuse, 28" wide, or ¼ yd. Timtex,
   22" wide, plus 1 yd. fusible web, 16" wide

2¼ yd. cording, ¹⁄₁₆" diameter

Large Box

1 fat quarter print 1 (box)

1 fat quarter print 2 (lid)

½ yd. print 3 (box lining, lid lining)

⅓ yd. Fast2Fuse, 28" wide, or ½ yd. Timtex,
   22" wide, plus 1½ yd. fusible web, 16" wide

3 yd. cording, ¹⁄₁₆" diameter

Other Supplies

Thread

Glue stick (optional)

Temporary spray adhesive (optional)

Cording foot for sewing machine (optional)

Heat- and steam-resistant shapes (optional)

General tools and supplies listed in Chapter 1

Note: If you are using a stiff interfacing with fusible web
already on both sides of it, omit the fusible web in the
supplies and cutting instructions. Disregard the reference
to fusible web in the construction steps. A glue stick or
temporary spray adhesive may be used in place of the
fusible web.

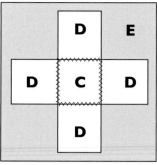

Lidded Cube Boxes —
Box Construction Diagram

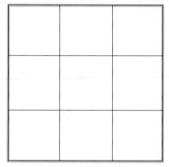

Lidded Cube Boxes —
Box Trimming & Cording Diagram

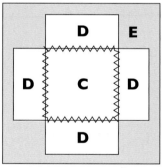

Lidded Cube Boxes —
Lid Construction Diagram

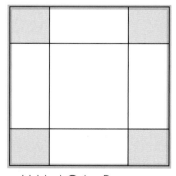

Lidded Cube Boxes —
Lid Trimming & Cording Diagram

Cut

Small Box

From	Size	How Many	For
Print 1	8½" x 8½"	1	Box, B
Print 2	6" x 6"	1	Lid, E
Print 3	8½" x 8½" 6" x 6"	1 1	Box lining, B Lid lining, E
Stiff interfacing	2½" x 2½" 2¾" x 2¾" 1¼" x 2¾"	5 1 4	Box bottom and sides, A Lid top, C Lid sides, D
Fusible web	8½" x 8½" 6" x 6"	2 2	Box, B Lid, E

Medium Box

From	Size	How Many	For
Print 1	11½" x 11½"	1	Box, B
Print 2	8" x 8"	1	Lid, E
Print 3	11½" x 11½" 8" x 8"	1 1	Box lining, B Lid lining, E
Stiff interfacing	3½" x 3½" 3¾" x 3¾" 1¾" x 3¾"	5 1 4	Box bottom and sides, A Lid top, C Lid sides, D
Fusible web	11½" x 11½" 8" x 8"	2 2	Box, B Lid, E

Large Box

From	Size	How Many	For
Print 1	14½" x 14½"	1	Box, B
Print 2	10" x 10"	1	Lid, E
Print 3	14½" x 14½" 10" x 10"	1 1	Box lining, B Lid lining, E
Stiff interfacing	4½" x 4½" 4¾" x 4¾" 2¼" x 4¾"	5 1 4	Box bottom and sides, A Lid top, C Lid sides, D
Fusible web	14½" x 14½" 10" x 10"	2 2	Box, B Lid, E

Construct

1. Follow the general Box Construction steps and the inside seam directions. Construct the box and lid.

2. Pink the flaps of the box seams to finish them.

3. Finish the lid seams by pinking the edges or completing the fold and tack technique.

4. Re-shape the box and lid.

Lidded In Boxes

Finished sizes:

Small box measures 9" x 12" x 3"; large box measures 9½" x 13½" x 3½".

The Lidded In Boxes feature inside seams. Fabrics provided by P&B Textiles;

decorative thread provided by Sulky of America.

Supplies
(for one box; same for small or large size)

1 fat quarter print 1 (box)
1 fat quarter print 2 (lid)
½ yd. print 3 (lid lining, box lining)
¾ yd. heavyweight Fast2Fuse, 28" wide,
   or 1 yd. Timtex, 22" wide, plus 2⅛ yd. lightweight
   fusible web, 16" wide
4½ yd. cording, ¹⁄₁₆" diameter
Thread
Glue stick (optional)
Temporary spray adhesive (optional)
Cording foot for machine (optional)
Heat- and steam-resistant shape (optional)
General tools and supplies listed in Chapter 1

Note: This project is best made with heavy-weight Fast2Fuse or standard-weight Timtex. If you are using a stiff interfacing with fusible web already on both sides of it, omit the fusible web in the supplies and cutting instructions. Disregard the reference to fusible web in the construction steps. A glue stick or temporary spray adhesive may be used in place of the fusible web.

Cut
Small Box

From	Size	How Many	For
Print 1	16" x 19"	1	Box, D
Print 2	14" x 17"	1	Lid, H
Print 3	16" x 19" 14" x 17"	1 1	Box lining, D Lid lining, H
Stiff interfacing	9" x 12" 3" x 9" 3" x 12" 9¼" x 12¼" 1¾" x 9¼" 1¾" x 12¼"	1 2 2 1 2 2	Box bottom, A Box sides, B Box sides, C Lid top, E Lid sides, F Lid sides, G
Fusible Web	16" x 19" 14" x 17"	2 2	Box, D Lid, H

Large Box

From	Size	How Many	For
Print 1	18" x 22"	1	Box, D
Print 2	15" x 19"	1	Lid, H
Print 3	18" x 22" 15" x 19"	1 1	Box lining, D Lid lining, H
Stiff interfacing	9½" x 13½" 3½" x 9½" 3½" x 13½" 9¾" x 13¾" 2" x 9¾" 2" x 13¾"	1 2 2 1 2 2	Box bottom, A Box sides, B Box sides, C Lid top, E Lid sides, F Lid sides, G
Fusible web	18" x 22" 15" x 19"	2 2	Box, D Lid, H

Construct

1. Follow the general Box Construction steps and the inside seam directions. Construct the box and lid; quilt both before sewing the side-seams to add stability. Refer to the same diagrams for both the box and lid.

2. Pink the flaps of the box and lid seams to finish them.

3. Re-shape the box and lid.

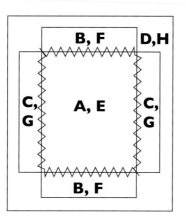

Lidded In Boxes –
Box and Lid Construction Diagram

TIP

Dress up your dinner table by making a fabric wrap for your favorite baking pan. The base of the large-size Lidded In Box is a perfect fit for a standard 9" × 13" baking pan.

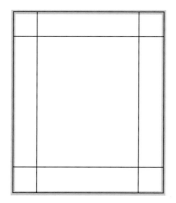

Lidded In Boxes –
Box and Lid
Trimming & Cording Diagram

Lidded Pen Organizer

Finished size: 2" x 4" x 7".
The Lidded Pen Organizer is constructed with outside seams,
and the lid has inside seams. Fabrics provided by P&B Textiles;
decorative thread provided by Sulky of America.

Supplies

½ yd. print 1 (box, lid)

½ yd. print 2 (box lining, lid lining)

⅓ yd. heavyweight Fast2Fuse, 28" wide, or ⅓ yd. Timtex, 22" wide, plus 1¾ yd. lightweight fusible web, 16" wide

3½ yd. cording, ¹⁄₁₆" diameter

Thread

Glue stick (optional)

Temporary spray adhesive (optional)

Cording foot for machine (optional)

Heat- and steam-resistant shape (optional)

General tools and supplies listed in Chapter 1

Note: This project is best made with heavyweight Fast2Fuse or standard-weight Timtex. If you are using a stiff interfacing with fusible web already on both sides of it, omit the fusible web in the supplies and cutting instructions, and disregard the reference to fusible web in the construction steps. A glue stick or temporary spray adhesive may be used in place of the fusible web.

Cut

From	Size	How Many	For
Print 1	17" x 19" 8" x 10"	1 1	Box, D Lid, G
Print 2	17" x 19" 8" x 10"	1 1	Box lining, D Lid lining, G
Stiff interfacing	2" x 4" 4" x 7" 2" x 7" 2¼" x 4¼" 2¼" x 2¼"	1 2 2 3 2	Box bottom, A Box sides, B Box sides, C Lid top and sides, E Lid sides, E
Fusible web	17" x 19" 8" x 10"	2 2	Box, D Lid, G

Construct

1. Follow the general Box Construction steps and the outside seam directions; construct the box.

2. Create the lid following the general Box Construction steps and the directions for inside seams.

3. Finish the lid seams using the pleat and wrap technique.

4. Re-shape the box and lid.

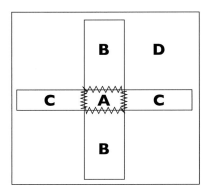

Lidded Pen Organizer –
Box Construction Diagram

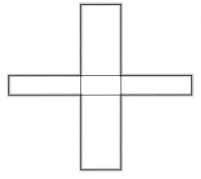

Lidded Pen Organizer –
Box Trimming & Cording Diagram

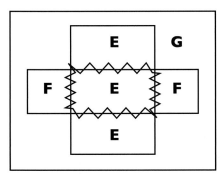

Lidded Pen Organizer –
Lid Construction Diagram

Lidded Pen Organizer –
Lid Trimming & Cording Diagram

TIP

Add a little beauty and inspiration to your work area. The pen box works great as a fabric vase to display your favorite dried or silk flowers.

TIP

Display your business cards in style. Make an extra box lid to keep your cards handy for customers!

Lidded Organizer

Finished size: 3" x 4" x 7".

This organizer is constructed with inside seams.

Fabrics provided by P&B Textiles; decorative thread provided by Sulky of America.

Supplies

1 fat quarter print 1 (box)

1 fat quarter print 2 (lid)

½ yd. print 3 (box lining, lid lining)

⅓ yd. Fast2Fuse, 28" wide, or ⅓ yd. Timtex, 22" wide, plus 1¼ yd. lightweight fusible web, 16" wide

3 yd. cording, ⅟₁₆" diameter

Thread

Glue stick (optional)

Temporary spray adhesive (optional)

Cording foot for machine (optional)

Heat- and steam-resistant shape (optional)

General tools and supplies listed in Chapter 1

Note: If you are using a stiff interfacing with fusible web already on both sides of it, omit the fusible web in the supplies and cutting instructions. Disregard the reference to fusible web in the construction steps. A glue stick or temporary spray adhesive may be used in place of the fusible web.

Cut

From	Size	How Many	For
Print 1	11" x 14"	1	Box
Print 2	8" x 11"	1	Lid
Print 3	11" x 14" 8" x 11"	1 1	Box lining Lid lining
Stiff interfacing	4" x 7" 3" x 7" 3" x 4" 4¼" x 7¼" 1½" x 7¼" 1½" x 4¼"	1 2 2 1 2 2	Box bottom Box sides Box sides Lid top Lid sides Lid sides
Fusible web	11" x 14" 8" x 11"	2 2	Box Lid

Construct

1. Follow the general Box Construction steps and the inside seam directions. Construct the box and lid.

2. Finish the box flaps with the pleat and wrap technique.

3. Finish the lid flaps with the fold and tack technique.

4. Re-shape the box and the lid.

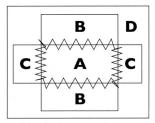

Lidded Organizer –
Box Construction Diagram

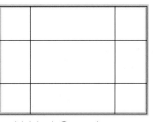

Lidded Organizer –
Box Trimming & Cording Diagram

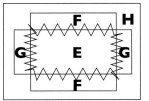

Lidded Organizer –
Lid Construction Diagram

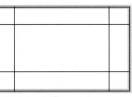

Lidded Organizer –
Lid Trimming & Cording Diagram

CHAPTER 4

Bowls

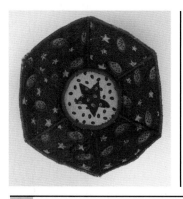

Start with fabric and thread, add stiff interfacing and round patterns and you have it… bowls! Make round or oval bowls in all different sizes, and even add some braided trim and handles. First, read the tips and general directions (and Tips for All Containers in Chapter 3), then jump into your first project. Have fun!

Tips for Bowls

• Find circle patterns in bucket lids, jar lids, tins, embroidery hoops and dinner plates. Oval shapes can be found in platters, wicker baskets and picture mats and frames.

• If your bowl pattern won't fit on one piece of tracing paper, tape two or more pieces together.

• Most bowls are reversible, allowing you to create two different looks in one project, so consider that as you choose your fabrics.

• Use a size 14/90 sewing machine needle if your standard-size needle breaks.

• If you are using a stiff interfacing that does not have fusible web on both sides of it, use a good quality glue stick, temporary spray adhesive or fusible web to attach fabric to the interfacing.

• Puckers form when you try to pull and tug too much as you sew the darts; be gentle and make small changes and adjustments as you sew.

• Begin stitching your dart from the inner base of your project, even if the dart starts ¾" away; sew it to the rim of the bowl. This stitching will add a nice line and focal point to your bowl.

• Sew the zigzag stitch on bowl darts using a foot that is physically shorter in length from front to back. The width of the foot doesn't matter as long as you can do a zigzag stitch with it. This shorter foot is easier to maneuver as you sew the darts.

• Experiment with decorative threads and quilting styles. Your thread and quilting can be as much a focus in the project as the fabrics used.

• Experiment by cutting different-size wedges in bowls for darts, thus changing the shape of the bowl.

• Cut and work on only one dart at a time to minimize fraying.

• Embellish the rim of your bowl with specialty yarns, beaded trims, individual beads or braided fabric strips as I have shown. Incorporate your other hobbies into your finished bowl.

- Add special quilting, embroidery or a fused design to the inner base; or, center a particular motif from a piece of fabric on this base.
- Bowls can be washed and dried using the settings appropriate for the fabrics within the project.
- With time or washings, you may need to re-shape your bowls. Steam press them, using steam-resistant shapes, such as glass mixing bowls or a tailor's ham, to re-form the bowl shape.
- Uses for bowls are as endless as the fabrics to make them. Let your imagination go wild, and consider them as both the container of other items and as a gift in themselves.

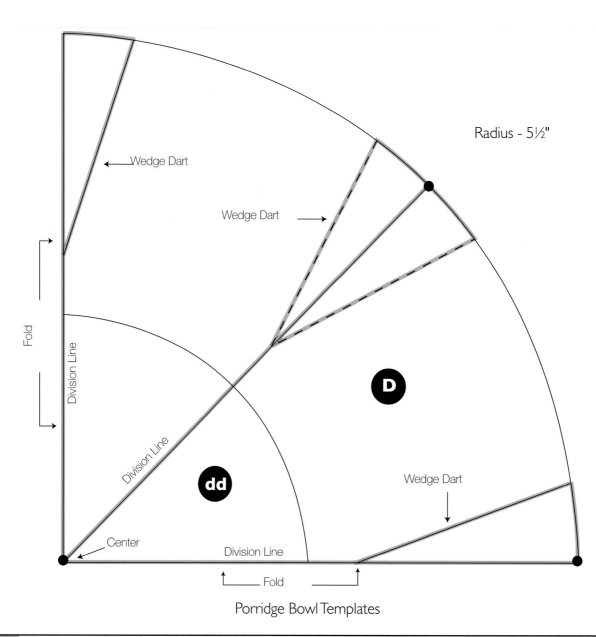

Porridge Bowl Templates

Bowl Construction

1. Fold a piece of tracing paper in half horizontally and again vertically. It is now one quarter its original size.

2. Match the fold lines from the paper with the fold lines marked on the template diagram for your particular project; trace the patterns for the bowl (marked with a single letter), inner base (marked with double letters) and all markings for your project onto the paper.

Note: The fabrics shown on pages 116-125 were provided by P&B Textiles. The decorative threads shown on pages 117-125 were provided by Sulky of America.

3. Cut out the bowl and inner base templates. The division lines (shown in blue) and dart wedges and curve cuts (shown in red) will be transferred to the project later.

TIP

Cut both the bowl and base shape from one paper. The hole in the center of the bowl shape will show you where to place the inner base.

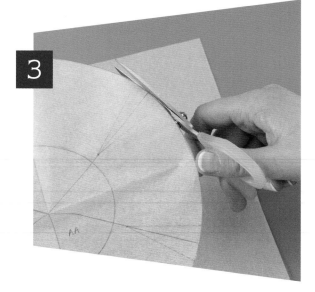

4. Cut the pieces as shown in the project. Use the templates you made in Step 1 to cut the stiff interfacing, fabric and fusible web (if applicable).

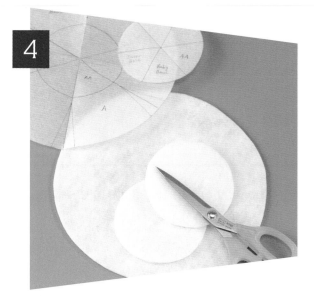

5. Follow the manufacturer's directions to iron fusible web pieces to the wrong side of the matching fabric pieces, unless specified otherwise. Remove all of the paper backing. Note: If you plan to use a glue stick or temporary spray adhesive with the Timtex interfacing, or if you are using Fast2Fuse, which already has fusible web on both of its sides, skip to Step 6.

6. Attach the selected bowl fabric to one side of a piece of stiff interfacing.

7. Trim the fabric even with bowl shape. Work with the interfacing side up, and use scissors or a small or medium-size rotary cutter to trim away the fabric.

8. Repeat Steps 5 through 7 for the second fabric on the reverse side of the bowl.

9. Repeat Steps 5 through 7 to complete the inner base shapes, adding fabric to one side only. If desired, quilt the bowl's inner base.

10. Refer to the template made in Step 1 and mark the division lines on one side of your bowl directly onto the fabric; use a chalk pencil, standard pencil or whatever will show up on your fabric. These lines define the segments or divisions of your bowl and show you where to make darts. Division lines are shown on your bowl templates in blue. The center point helps position the inner base of your bowl properly. If desired, mark faint and removable lines on the inner base near the outer raw edge.

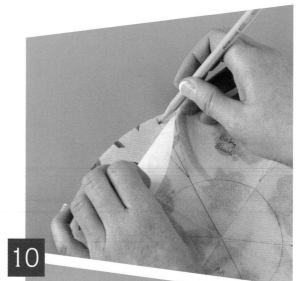

11. Attach one inner base (fabric side up) to the center point of bowl; use glue stick or temporary spray adhesive.

12. Use a straight stitch to sew around the inner base piece, but not on it. This will mark the position of the base on the other side of your bowl, and it will be covered by other stitching.

13. Attach the second inner base (fabric side up) to the reverse side of the bowl, centering it inside the stitching lines.

14. Satin stitch around the raw edge of the inner base with matching, contrasting or decorative thread. Work from one side and sew through the inner base and bowl. Refer to the Machine Settings Table on page 121 for suggested settings. Test your settings on scraps of interfacing; be sure to note the best settings for your machine in the space provided.

15. Turn the bowl over. Sew a satin stitch over the previous stitching as you work from this side; use a wider and tighter zigzag stitch. Refer to the Machine Settings Table.

16. Quilt the bowl while it is still flat in whatever style you wish; quilt up to but not on the inner base. The inner bases should have been quilted before this, if at all.) If you prefer to have a certain quilting design in each section of the bowl, put this in the open area between the drawn division lines.

TIP

Experiment with your machine quilting. Play with a variety of threads, use decorative stitches on your machine, or even match your quilting to a fabric or theme.

Quilting Designs

MACHINE SETTINGS TABLE

Suggested Starting Zigzag Settings

Use these settings as a starting point to determine the best zigzag stitch needed for your machine and fabrics. Make a test piece using the same materials to find what works best. If one round of stitching covers nicely, skip the second round.

1. First round of zigzag stitching (sometimes stitched over cording)

Stitch length = ½

Stitch width = 3½

2. Second round of zigzag stitching sewn over the first stitches (called a satin stitch; without cording)

Stitch length = ⅜

Stitch width = 4¼

Your Machine's Best Zigzag Settings

As you complete some test stitching and tweak your machine's settings, it will become clear what zigzag stitch lengths and widths work the best. Jot down that information below for your handy reference.

Date: ____________________ Your Machine Type: ______________________________

First round zigzag stitching

Stitch length: ______________________________

Stitch width: ______________________________

Second round zigzag stitching

Stitch length: ______________________________

Stitch width: ______________________________

17. Mark the darts (shown in red on the original diagram) at each division line; mark these directly on your bowl fabric using a marking tool that works for your fabric. Trace wedge shapes or draw random gentle curves, depending on the dart. Drawn lines should be ¼" or more away from the inner base.

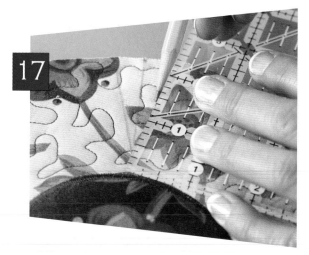

18. Create the darts desired for your bowl. For overlapping darts, complete Steps 19 through 22. To create wedge darts, complete Steps 23 through 26.

> ### TIP
>
> Sew all of the darts once (first round of zigzag stitching) to make sure you like the bowl's shape. If needed, make adjustments at this point. Then, go back and sew the second round of zigzag stitching (the satin stitch) over each dart seam to give each line a finished look.

OVERLAPPING DARTS

19. To begin an overlapping dart, make a gentle, free-form cut over one division line beginning at the rim; a sample curve has been drawn on your template as a guide, but you can try other curves. Cut only one curve, and work on one overlapping dart at a time.

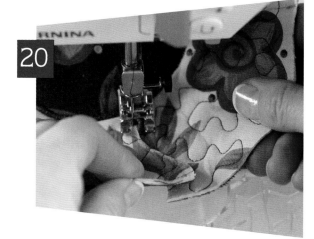

20. Form the dart by overlapping the raw edges of this cut, pulling and tugging gently to overlap edges. Stitch with a loose zigzag stitch from the inner base to the rim. Backstitch at the beginning and end of stitching. Refer to the Machine Settings Table for detailed information.

21. Turn the bowl over, and stitch the visible raw edge of the dart in the same manner. Repeat for each bowl division. Overlap the same amount at each interval for a uniform bowl shape.

22. To finish the darts, sew a second, tighter zig-zag stitch on top of the first line of stitching. Refer to the Machine Settings Table for detailed information. Note: This dart method creates two raw edges to satin stitch (another design element), but it also takes more time and thread. Go to Step 27.

WEDGE DARTS

23. To begin a wedge dart, mark a wedge shape at each bowl division; use the wedge template provided or create your own.

TIP

If your first round of stitching covers the darts nicely and looks professional, there is no need to stitch a second round.

24. Cut only one wedge and work on only one dart at a time.

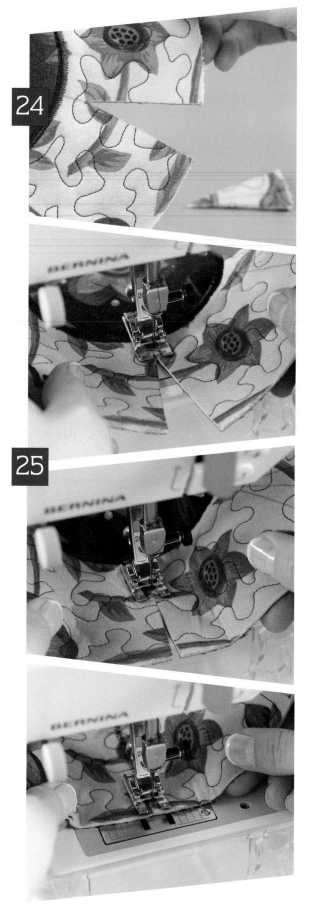

25. Form the wedge dart by gently pushing together raw edges of the cut area. The edges will butt up to each other, but they do not overlap, creating a "line" where they touch. Sew a loose zigzag stitch that is centered over this "line." Sew from the inner base to the rim of the bowl and backstitch at beginning and end. Repeat Steps 23 through 25 for each bowl division. Refer to the Machine Settings Table for detailed information.

26. To finish the darts, sew a second tighter zig-zag stitch (satin stitch) on top of the first stitching; refer to the Machine Settings Table for detailed information.

TIP

Use a cording foot on the upper rim of the bowl projects; this presser foot (pictured in Step 28) is designed to simplify sewing with cording or thick yarn. Cording feeds through a hole in the foot, and grooves consistently guide it under the needle in the same position. Why add cording to your project in the first place? The edges finish nicer with cording, and it usually takes less thread for coverage.

27. If needed, trim the upper edge of the bowl to straighten out any unwanted curves. Trim all of the threads.

28. Use a cording foot (optional) to add cording and finish the bowl's upper edges; work from the right side of your project. Refer to the Machine Settings Table for detailed information. Zigzag stitch over the cording as you add it to the upper rim of your project. Use a thread to match or contrast your project. This may or may not cover the cording.

29. Repeat Step 28 if needed; sew over the previous zigzag stitching, but this time, skip the cording and use a tighter and wider stitch. This second row of zigzag stitching (a satin stitch) should completely cover the cording and give the bowl a professional appearance.

30. Shape the finished project using steam and a heat- and steam-resistant form, such as a tailor's ham or a glass mixing bowl.

31. Embellish the finished bowl as desired.

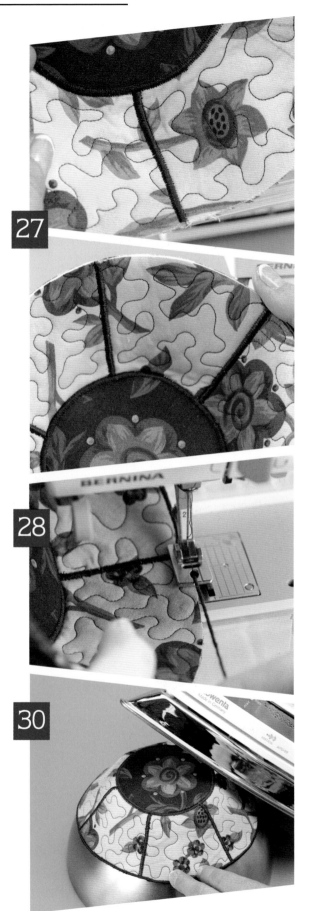

Round Bowls

Finished sizes:

Baby Bowl is 6½" in diameter and 2" deep;

Mama Bowl is 8½" in diameter and 2¼" deep;

and Papa Bowl is 10" in diameter and 2½" deep.

Supplies (for one bowl)

Baby Bowl

1 fat quarter print fabric 1 (bowl, inner base)

1 fat quarter print fabric 2 (reverse side of bowl, inner base)

¼ yd. Fast2Fuse, 28" wide; or ¼ yd. Timtex, 22" wide plus ½ yd. lightweight fusible web, 16" wide

1 yd. cording, ¹⁄₁₆" diameter

Tracing or other lightweight paper, 9" × 9"

Mama Bowl

1 fat quarter print fabric 1 (bowl, inner base)

1 fat quarter print fabric 2 (reverse side of bowl, inner base)

⅓ yd. Fast2Fuse, 28" wide; or ⅓ yd. Timtex, 22" wide plus ¾ yd. lightweight fusible web, 16" wide

1⅛ yd. cording, ¹⁄₁₆" diameter

Tracing or other lightweight paper, 11" × 11"

Papa Bowl

1 fat quarter fabric 1 (bowl, inner base)

1 fat quarter fabric 2 (reverse side of bowl, inner base)

⅜ yd. Fast2Fuse, 28" wide; or ⅜ yd. Timtex, 22" wide plus ¾ yd. lightweight fusible web, 16" wide

1½ yd. cording, ¹⁄₁₆" diameter

Tracing or other lightweight paper, 12" × 12"

Other supplies

Thread

Glue stick

Temporary spray adhesive (optional)

Cording foot for machine (optional)

General tools and supplies listed in Chapter 1

Note: If you are using a stiff interfacing with fusible web already on both sides of it, omit the fusible web in the supply list and cutting instructions, and disregard the reference to fusible web in the construction steps. A glue stick or temporary spray adhesive may be used in place of the fusible web. Refer to Tips for Bowls and Bowl Construction.

Cut

Baby Bowl

From	Size	How Many	For
Fabric 1	9" x 9" 4" x 4"	1 1	Bowl Inner base
Fabric 2	9" x 9" 4" x 4"	1 1	Bowl reverse Inner base reverse
Stiff interfacing	Template A Template aa	1 2	Bowl Inner base
Fusible web	Template A Template aa	2 2	Bowl Inner base

Mama Bowl

From	Cut	How Many	For
Fabric 1	10½" x 10½" 4½" x 4½"	1 1	Bowl Inner base
Fabric 2	10½" x 10½" 4½" x 4½"	1 1	Bowl reverse Inner base reverse
Stiff interfacing	Template B Template bb	1 2	Bowl Inner base
Fusible web	Template B Template bb	2 2	Bowl Inner base

Papa Bowl

From	Cut	How Many	For
Fabric 1	12½" x 12½" 6" x 6"	1 1	Bowl Inner base
Fabric 2	12½" x 12½" 6" x 6"	1 1	Bowl reverse Inner base reverse
Stiff interfacing	Template C Template cc	1 2	Bowl Inner base
Fusible web	Template C Template cc	2 2	Bowl Inner base

Construct

Each bowl is divided into six equal parts and is reversible.

1. Baby Bowl: Follow the general Bowl Construction steps and the wedge dart directions. Find the templates on page 130.

2. Mama Bowl: Follow the general Bowl Construction steps and the overlapping dart directions. Find the templates on page 130.

3. Papa Bowl: Follow the general Bowl Construction steps and the overlapping dart directions. Find the templates on page 131.

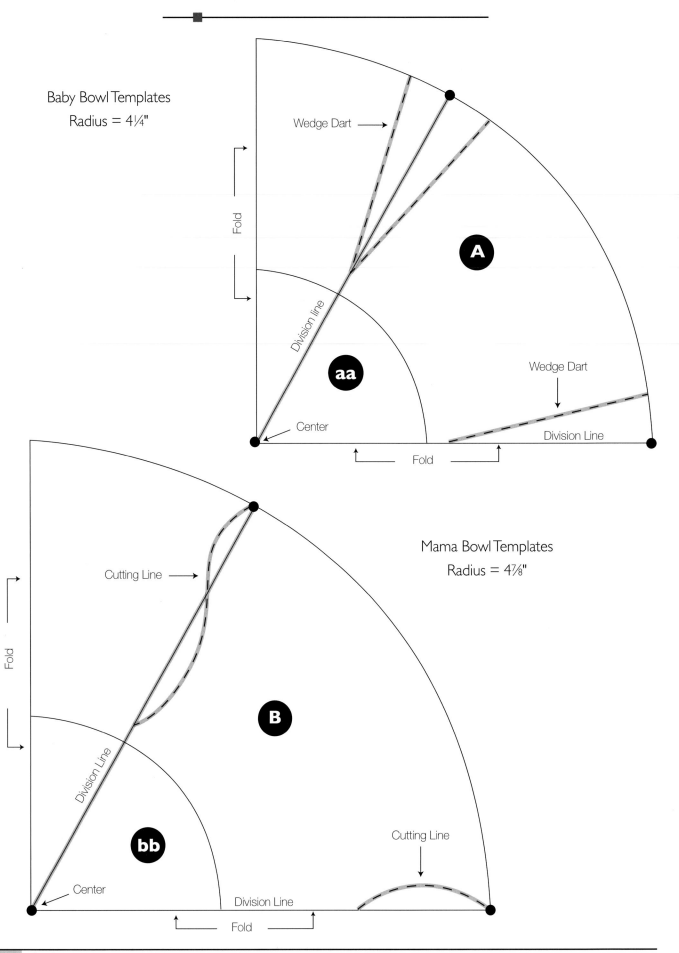

Baby Bowl Templates
Radius = 4¼"

Wedge Dart

A

Fold

Division line

aa

Center

Wedge Dart

Fold

Division Line

Cutting Line

B

Fold

Division Line

bb

Mama Bowl Templates
Radius = 4⅞"

Cutting Line

Center

Division Line

Fold

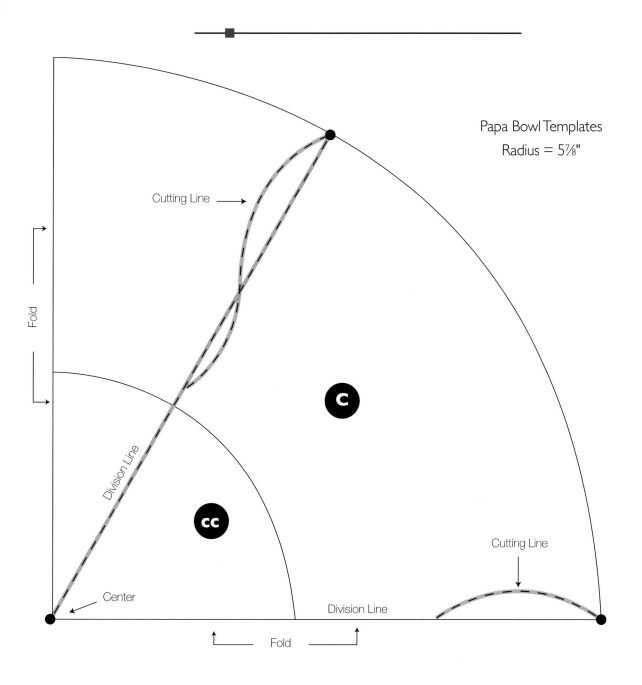

Papa Bowl Templates
Radius = 5⅞"

Cutting Line

Fold

Cutting Line

C

Division Line

cc

Center

Division Line

Fold

Porridge Bowl with Braided Trim

Finished size: 8" in diameter and 2¾" deep.

This deep-dish bowl features braided fabric trim around the upper rim.

Supplies

⅝ yd. multicolored print fabric 1
  (bowl, inner bases, braid)
1 fat quarter blue print fabric 2 (bowl reverse)
⅓ yd. Fast2Fuse, 28" wide; or ⅓ yd. Timtex, 22"
  wide, plus ⅔ yd. lightweight fusible web, 16" wide
1 yd. cording, 1/16" diameter
Thread
Tracing paper or other lightweight paper, 12" x 12"
Small clamp, office clips, safety pins
Glue stick
Temporary spray adhesive (optional)
Cording foot for machine (optional)
Heat- and steam-resistant shape (optional)
General tools and supplies listed in Chapter 1

Note: If you are using a stiff interfacing with fusible web already on both sides of it, omit fusible web in the supply list and cutting instructions, and disregard the references to fusible web in the construction steps. A glue stick or temporary spray adhesive may be used in place of the fusible web.

Cut

From	Size	How Many	For
Fabric 1	1"-wide strips	6	Braid
	11½" x 11½"	1	Bowl, D
	5½" x 5½"	2	Inner base, dd
Fabric 2	11½" x 11½"	1	Bowl reverse, D
Stiff interfacing	Template D	1	Bowl, D
	Template dd	2	Inner base
Fusible web	11½" x 11½"	2	Bowl
	5½" x 5½"	2	Inner base

Construct

The Porridge Bowl is divided into eight equal parts. It is not reversible because of the braid trim. Find the templates on page 114.

1. Follow the general Bowl Construction steps and the wedge dart directions.

2. Make at least 28" of finished braid. For detailed instructions, refer to Chapter 1.

3. Attach the braid to rim of the bowl by hand or machine.

Oval Bowls with Braided Handles

Finished sizes:

Small Bowl, 6½" × 9" and 3" deep; Large Bowl, 8½" × 11" and 3¼" deep.

Both of these oval bowls are made with wedge darts and have braided trim and handles.

Supplies (for one bowl)
Small Bowl
⅝ yd. fabric 1 (bowl, inner base, braid trim)

½ yd. fabric 2 (bowl reverse, inner base reverse)

⅓ yd. Fast2Fuse, 28" wide, or ⅓ yd. Timtex, 22" wide, plus ⅞ yd. lightweight fusible web, 16" wide

Tracing paper or other lightweight paper, 11" x 13"

1 yd. cording, 1/16" diameter

Large Bowl
¾ yd. fabric 1 (bowl, inner base, braid trim)

⅝ yd. fabric 2 (bowl reverse, inner base reverse)

½ yd. Fast2Fuse, 28" wide, or ½ yd. Timtex, 22" wide, plus 1¼ yd. lightweight fusible web, 16" wide

Tracing paper or other lightweight paper, 12" x 15"

1½ yd. cording, 1/16" diameter

Other Supplies
Thread

Glue stick

Temporary spray adhesive (optional)

Small clamp, office clips, safety pins (braid)

Cording foot for machine (optional)

Heat- and steam-resistant shape (optional)

General tools and supplies listed in Chapter 1

Note: If you are using a stiff interfacing with fusible web already on both sides of it, omit the fusible web in the supply list and cutting instructions, and disregard the references to fusible web in the construction steps. A glue stick or temporary spray adhesive may be used in place of the fusible web.

TIP

For a faster finish and different look, make the bowl without the braided handles.

Cut
Small Bowl

From	Size	How Many	For
Fabric 1	1½"-wide strips 11" x 13" 4½" x 6½"	4 1 1	Braid Bowl, C Inner base
Fabric 2	1½"-wide strips 11" x 13" 4½" x 6½"	2 1 1	Braid Bowl Inner base
Stiff interfacing	Template A Template aa	1 2	Bowl Inner base
Fusible web	11" x 13" 4½" x 6½"	2 2	Bowl Inner base

Large Bowl

From	Size	How Many	For
Fabric 1	2"-wide strips	4	Braid
	12½" x 14½"	1	Bowl
	6" x 8"	1	Inner base
Fabric 2	2"-wide strips	2	Braid
	11" x 18"	1	Bowl
	6" x 8"	1	Inner base
Stiff interfacing	Template B	1	Bowl
	Template bb	2	Inner base
Fusible web	11" x 18"	2	Bowl
	6" x 8"	2	Inner base

Construct

Each bowl is divided into eight equal parts and is not reversible because of the braid handles and trim.

1. Small Bowl: Follow the general Bowl Construction steps and the wedge dart directions.

2. Large Bowl: Follow the general Bowl Construction steps and the wedge dart directions.

3. Small Bowl Trim and Handles: Make at least 26" of braided trim for the rim of the bowl and 13" of braided trim for the handles (two 6½" pieces). For detailed instructions, refer to Chapter 1. Attach the braided trim to the rim of the bowl by hand or machine; add the handles in the same way.

4. Large Bowl Trim and Handles: Make at least 32" of braided trim for the rim of bowl and 14" total of braided trim for the handles (two 7" pieces). For detailed instructions, refer to Chapter 1. Attach the braided trim to the rim of the bowl by hand or machine; add the handles in the same way.

Turn leftover fabric into useful accessories. Depending on how much fabric you have left, you can create braided napkin rings, trivets or placemats. For a napkin ring, simply join the ends of a finished length of braided trim. (A 7" braid was used here.)

To create a coaster, trivet or place mat, join lengths of braided trim and coil them into the desired shape and size, tacking the strips together frequently to hold the shape.

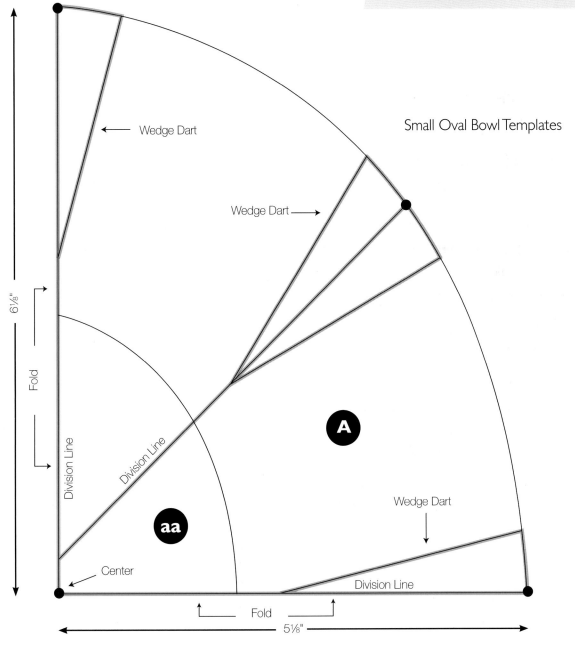

Wedge Dart

Wedge Dart

Small Oval Bowl Templates

6⅛"

Fold

Division Line

Division Line

A

aa

Wedge Dart

Center

Division Line

Fold

5⅛"

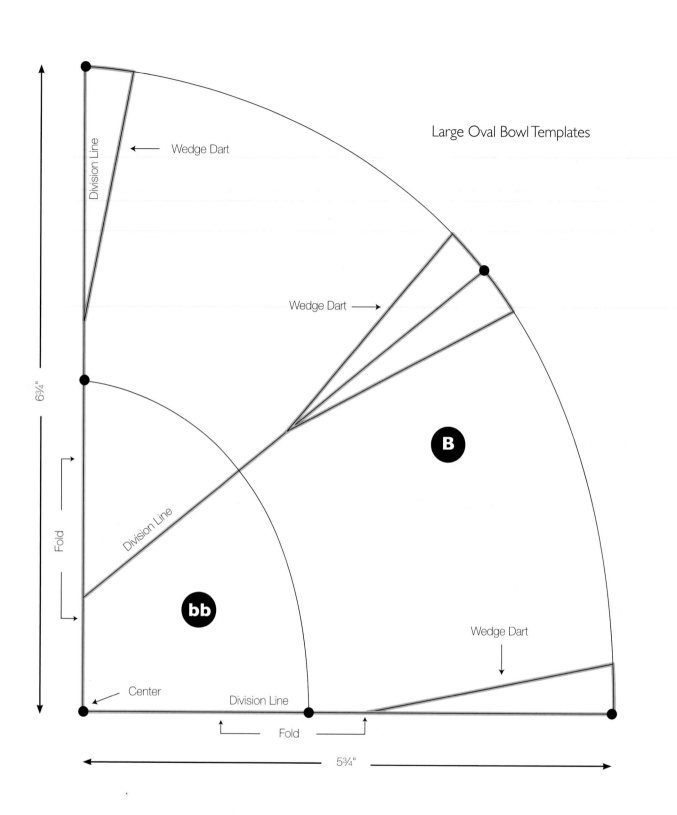

Large Oval Bowl Templates

Division Line

Wedge Dart

Wedge Dart

Wedge Dart

6¾"

Fold

Division Line

B

bb

Center

Division Line

Fold

5¾"

Hexagon Bowl

Finished size:
5" in diameter and 2" deep. This bowl is constructed
the same as the Round Bowls, and it is made with wedge darts. Fabrics by P&B Textiles.

Supplies

1 fat quarter fabric 1 (bowl, inner base)

1 fat quarter fabric 2
  (bowl reverse, inner base reverse)

⅓ yd. Fast2Fuse, 28" wide, or ⅓ yd. Timtex,
  22" wide, plus ⅝ yd. lightweight fusible web,
  16" wide

1½ yd. cording, ¹⁄₁₆" diameter

Thread

Tracing paper or other lightweight paper, 8½" x 11"

Glue stick

Temporary spray adhesive (optional)

Cording foot for machine (optional)

Heat- and steam-resistant shape (optional)

General tools and supplies listed in Chapter 1

Note: If you are using a stiff interfacing with fusible web already on both sides of it, omit the fusible web in the supply list and cutting instructions, and disregard the references to fusible web in the construction steps. A glue stick or temporary spray adhesive may be used in place of the fusible web.

TIP

Select novelty prints for the bowl, and fussy cut the inner base fabric as a focal point.

Cut

From	Size	How Many	For
Fabric 1	9" x 10" 3½" x 3½"	1 1	Bowl Inner base
Fabric 2	9" x 10" 3½" x 3½"	1 1	Bowl reverse Inner base reverse
Stiff interfacing	Template A Template aa	1 2	Bowl Inner base
Fusible web	9" x 10" 3½" x 3½"	2 2	Bowl Fusible web

Construct

The construction of a hexagon-shaped bowl is the same as a round bowl, even though a hexagon is the beginning base here. The bowl is divided into six equal parts and is reversible.

1. Follow the general Bowl Construction steps and the wedge dart directions. In Step 1, fold the template in half once before tracing the elements; the diagram is shown half of the finished size.

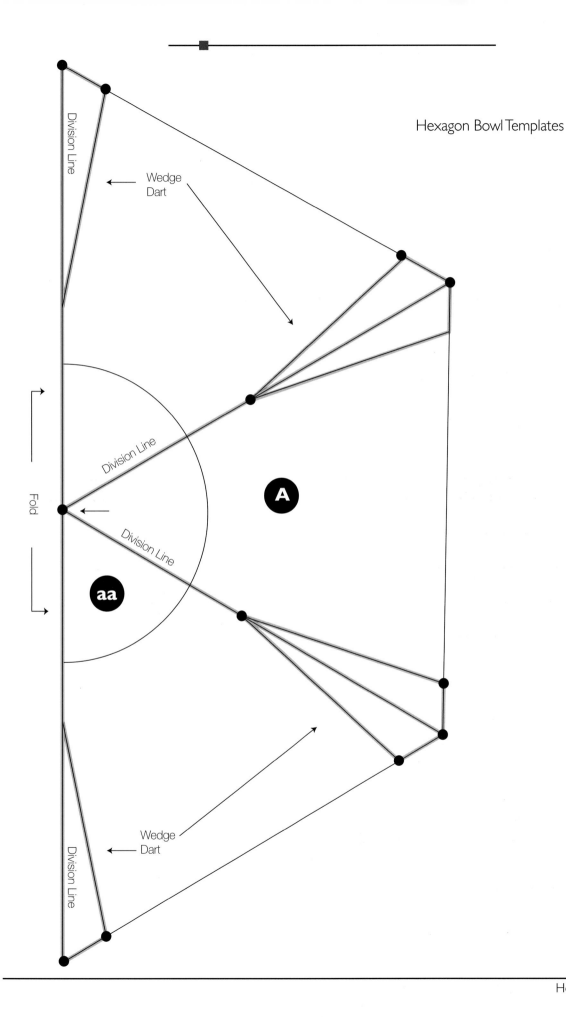

Hexagon Bowl Templates

Division Line

Wedge
Dart

Fold

Division Line

Division Line

A

aa

Wedge
Dart

Division Line

Division Line

GLOSSARY

Audition fabric — To actually lay out the fabrics chosen for a project to see if the combination is as effective as you want. This is often done by overlapping fabrics, with more fabric showing for pieces that will be cut a larger size than others. Auditioning is also done to test how a certain combination will look when braided or woven.

Cording Foot — A sewing machine presser foot designed to simplify sewing with cording or thick yarn. Cording feeds through a hole in the foot, and grooves guide it under the needle consistently in the same position.

Fat Quarter — A piece of fabric that measures approximately 18" x 22". It starts as a half-yard cut of fabric that is cut again at the fold or halfway point.

Finished Size — The size of an item after all seams have been sewn. Note that the calculated finished size doesn't necessarily match the sewn finished size.

Fusible or Fusible Web — A flat, dry, glue product used to attach two fabrics or other items together, often with paper on one side or both sides, and/or a glue substance on the other. Most often, fusible web is ironed to make the fusing permanent. Several varieties are available, each with unique characteristics and specific instructions for use.

Fussy Cut — To cut a required size and shape, but to specifically center a design of the fabric in that shape. Fussy cutting often is done with novelty prints or large motifs.

Grain of Fabric — The direction of the fabric weave. The straight of grain is parallel to the selvage. Fabric on the straight of grain is the strongest and allows the least amount of stretch. The bias grain of the fabric is at a 45-degree angle to the selvage. Fabric is weakest along the bias, which allows the most stretch and is easily distorted. The cross-grain of fabric is the grain at a 90-degree angle to the selvage. The cross-grain of fabric allows some stretch, and it can be distorted. When you are directed to cut strips of fabric, you most often cut on the cross-grain (selvage to selvage) for economy of fabric.

Round — Hooking in a circular pattern (clockwise or counterclockwise) around a certain area or around the canvas perimeter. For example, three rounds means you will hook around the project three times, like jogging around a track three times.

Row — Hooking in a back-and-forth motion where each line of stitching is a single row. Think of this as pacing back and forth, right to left.

Satin Stitch — A very close zigzag stitch made by machine; the width varies by project. Begin with a standard zigzag stitch and gradually shorten the stitch length; if stitching starts bunching up on top of itself, lengthen the stitch slightly.

Strip — A strip of fabric cut on the cross-grain. Strips most often are cut from selvage to selvage to make a piece that is the specified width and measures approximately 40" to 44" long.

Twine — Resembling strong cotton string, twine is used in locker hooking to anchor the fabric.

Wrap — A term used in tassel making. A wrap is a complete circle around a given-size piece of cardboard; several wraps are needed to make a tassel. Wrap also refers to the single layer of threads that encircle the upper edge of a tassel.

Support your local quilt or craft shop where you will find most of the fabrics, threads, rulers, and other supplies used to make these projects. Information listings were correct at the time of publication.

Bernina of America, Inc.
Manufacturer of sewing machines
3702 Prairie Lake Court
Aurora, IL 60504
Phone: (630) 978-2500
Web: www.berninausa.com

Clover Needlecraft, Inc.
Sewing and quilting notions
13438 Alondra Blvd.
Cerritos, CA 90703
E-mail: cni@clover-usa.com
Web: www.clover-usa.com

DMC Inc.
Embroidery floss
South Hackensack Avenue
Port Kearny Building 10F
South Kearny, NJ 07032
Phone: (973) 589-0606
Web: www.dmc-usa.com

Fast2Fuse Interfacing
Double-sided fusible stiff interfacing
Available at local retailers or from C&T Publishing
1651 Challenge Drive
Concord, CA 94520-5206
(800) 284-1114 (U.S.)
(925) 677-0377 (international)
E-mail: ctinfo@ctpub.com
Web: www.fast2fuse.com or www.ctpub.com

Furniture and Appliancemart Superstore
Retailer of name-brand furniture, appliances, electronics and bedding, and provider of photo shoot location
3349 Church St.
Stevens Point, WI 54481
Phone: (715) 344-7700
Web: www.furnitureappliancemart.com

June Tailor
Assorted sewing and quilting notions and tools
P.O. Box 208
Richfield, WI 53076
Phone: (800) 844-5400
E-mail: customerservice@junetailor.com
Web: www.junetailor.com

Krause Publications
Publisher of this and other quality how-to books for sewing, quilting, machine embroidery and other crafts
700 E. State St.
Iola, WI 54990-0001
Phone: (888) 457-2873
Web: www.krause.com

M.C.G. Textiles
Locker hooking kits and supplies, including Graph 'n' Latch Canvas, locker hooks, and twine used for projects in this book
596 Crane St.
Lake Elsinore, CA 92530
Phone: (951) 674-1350
Web: www.mcgtextiles.com

Moose Country Quilts
Featuring patterns, classes and catalogs by author Terrie Kralik
P.O. Box 902
Bonners Ferry, ID 83805
Phone: (208) 267-0713
E-mail: moosequilts@hotmail.com
Web: www.moosecountryquilts.com

P&B Textiles
Manufacturer of fabrics to inspire you, including fabrics used for several projects in this book
Web: www.pbtex.com

Prym Consumer USA
Sewing, quilting, cutting and craft-related tools and notions
P.O. Box 5028
Spartanburg, SC 29304
Web: www.dritz.com

Rowenta
Steamers and irons
196 Boston Ave.
Medford, MA 02155
Phone: (781) 396-0600
Web: www.rowenta.com

Schmetz
Sewing machine needles
Web: www.schmetz.com

Sulky of America, Inc.
Manufacturer of threads, stabilizers and spray adhesives, including many decorative threads used for several projects in this book
Phone: (800) 874-4115 (to obtain a mail-order source)
Web: www.sulky.com

Timber Lane Press
Timtex stiff interfacing, which was provided for the projects in this book, is made exclusively for this company, which will take wholesale orders or recommend retail outlets
24350 N. Rimrock Road
Hayden, ID 83835
(208) 765-3353
(800) 752-3353 (wholesale orders only)
E-mail: qltblox@earthlink.net

The Warm Co.
Batting and fusible products used in many of the projects in this book, including Lite Steam-a-Seam and Lite Steam-A-Seam 2
954 E. Union St.
Seattle, WA 98122
Phone: (800) 234-9276
E-mail: info@warmcompany.com
Web: www.warmcompany.com

Wrights
EZ Quilting tools, trims, embellishments and rayon cording
85 South St.
P.O. Box 398
West Warren, MA 01092
Phone: (800) 660-0415
Web: www.wrights.com or www.ezquilt.com

Additional Resources

Annie's Attic
Web: www.anniesattic.com

Baby Lock
Web: www.babylock.com

Bernina of America
Web: www.berninausa.com

Brother
Web: www.brother-usa.com

Clotilde LLC
Web: www.clotilde.com

Connecting Threads
Web: www.ConnectingThreads.com

Elna USA
Web: www.elnausa.com

Ghee's
Web: www.ghees.com

Herrschners Inc.
Web: www.herrschners.com

Home Sew
Web: www.homesew.com

Husqvarna Viking Sewing Machine Co.
Web: www.husqvarnaviking.com

Janome
Web: www.janome.com

Keepsake Quilting
Web: www.keepsakequilting.com

Kenmore
Web: www.sears.com

Nancy's Notions
Web: www.nancysnotions.com

Olfa-North America
Web: www.olfarotary.com

Pfaff
Web: www.pfaffusa.com

Singer
Web: www.singerco.com

Tacony Corp.
Web: www.tacony.com

The Timtex Store
Web: www.timtexstore.com

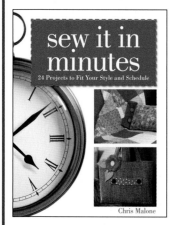
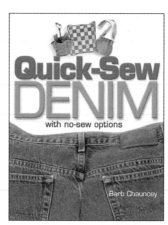
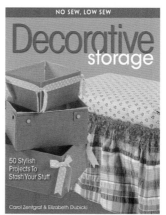